The Big Day

THE ULTIMATE LIFE COACHING SERIES

Volume 1

The How-to Guide
for Creating a Culture of
Physically, Mentally, Emotionally & Spiritually
Successful Leaders

ROBERT W. WHIPPLE

published by

D1497032

The Big Day

Cover design by Yvonne Avila
Edited by Heather Lester / The Big Day®: info@readyforthebigday.com
Edited by Blake Atwood / BA Writing Solutions LLC: BlakeAtwood.com

Paperback ISBN 13: 9780999279809
Ebook ISBN 13: 9780999279816

TABLE OF CONTENTS

Important Operating Instructions

for *The Big Day*

ATTENTION: You need to closely read these operating instructions and follow them diligently for this manual to produce optimal results.

Do not rely on your willpower or intellect to fully comprehend this phenomenal life-coaching manual. Ask God to help you by opening the eyes of your understanding to His wisdom. Ask Him to help you see what you need to see, and specifically ask Him to give you the strength, courage, and discipline to do what you need to do in order to rise to new heights.

Please don't read this manual just to say you have read it. Slowly reread each chapter several times. Study and reflect on the concepts of every chapter before moving on to the next chapter. Then comes the fun part: practice the concepts and exercises no matter how simple they may be! Each of these chapters possesses a college semester's worth of teaching principles, as if you were pursuing your MBA in life and progressing to the next level in every area.

As you evaluate your life, don't be too tough on yourself. Recognize what needs to change and start making small changes daily, no matter where you are starting from right now. It's the small, positive changes you make each day that produce life-changing transformations.

If there is something in this manual that you don't necessarily agree with or you do not understand, that's absolutely OK. There are many books (actually, almost every book, except the Bible) in which I have read certain things that I didn't necessarily agree with, but that doesn't mean the book didn't have good information that helped me or even changed my life for the better.

Also, please do not be offended at some of the things that are written. It's going to be a little tough, but as a life coach, my job is to kick some tail and teach, train, and especially encourage. Even to this day, I'm still working on myself too.

After reading halfway through the book, if you believe it is already helping you in a significant way, then buy several copies and give them to the people you care about. It's one of the best seeds you can plant in their lives.

I've written this guide as a personal life coach designed to help you become the most physically, mentally, emotionally, and spiritually successful leader of *you* that you can be. That's why I am convinced that the content covered here will be a game changer for millions of people. Thus, together we will create a culture of successful leaders. Culture always starts small. But as the number of people who adopt the same mentality and identity increases, that culture begins to set in and grow. The same idea is true here. A culture of successful leadership starts with one person, just like you or me, who decides to turn the "average" day into *the big day*, making the most of every moment, every experience, and every opportunity. As you and I do the small things right consistently, as we align our thoughts, emotions, and perspectives with the wisdom of God, then the people in our sphere of influence will see our quality of life improving, and they will naturally want the same kind of life-transformation for themselves.

In other words, winning big is contagious. When enough of us decide to tap into our God-given potential, we will see our paradigm shift turn into a culture shift. Then it won't be just you and me living successful lives; it will be all of us. That's the goal of *The Big Day*.

Considering this, I encourage you to start group studies every week or two weeks to discuss and analyze the concepts, ideas, and principles given and how they relate to your life. Encourage each other and keep each other accountable along the way. As you do, remember: don't rush through it. Instead, make the most of it all.

I thank God for the opportunity to write *The Big Day*. It has been in the making for over twenty-five years. Even though I may not know you by name, I will be praying for every single person reading this book. I pray you will read it with an open mind and an open heart, that you will be the best you can be in this life, and, most importantly, reach your highest potential of where you will spend eternity.

"For I know the thoughts that I think toward you, says the Lord, thoughts of peace and not of evil, to give you a future and a hope" (Jeremiah 29:11 NKJV).

Section One

SETTING UP FOR SUCCESS

CHAPTER ONE

Getting Started

Great accomplishments start with great commitments. Sometimes, the most critical aspect of a great commitment is *just showing up and getting started*. Did you know that your commitment has power? It does! Never underestimate the power of getting started on your commitments *today*.

Let this book serve as your personal coach.

Beyond a shadow of a doubt, I firmly believe that this book has the basic steps and articulated, practical information that can serve as your wake-up call for a life of adventure and excellence. This book is designed to help you take your life as it is now, whatever it looks like, and shape it into an awesome testimony of greatness. It's about helping you reach your high calling as a light on a hill[1] for all to see — a bright, bright light! And what exactly does it mean to be a bright light? It means that your physical, mental, emotional, and spiritual health is a living testimony and mentor to all who see you. How do you do this? By simply walking the talk (doing what you say you're going to do), both in the natural and in the spiritual.

Throughout the book, you will notice a variety of tools and strategies to help you overcome life's challenges and setbacks and to coach you in your journey to greatness. At the end of each chapter, I've written *keynotes* (main points) for that chapter. Take the time to read through them. Also, you'll find *checklists*, which are lists of crucial points to remember and serve many different purposes. I would even encourage you to use them as examples of how to create checklists for yourself. Utilizing checklists will keep you focused on the task at hand by quickly putting you back on track when you get distracted. In this way, checklists help you stay efficient with your time. They also keep you from forgetting what's important and even necessary in some cases. You will soon see why.

13

If you're reading this book, you are probably like a great number of people I have met: in addition to living a fulfilling life, you also want to succeed in whatever you do. Whether you're a stay-at-home parent or a CEO; whether you're a student, an athlete, a pastor, or the president of an organization; whether you're in an entry-level job, in mid-level management, or you're a sales professional — whatever your profession or goal in life may be, the goal is to *win big*, not to lead a life of Mr. and Mrs. Average or Below Average. There's more for you than that!

Who is Robert Whipple?

I've been asked numerous times by some of my wise team members to explain who Robert Whipple is to our readers, so I would like to honor their request.

Like most of us, I relate best to stories whether they're true or fictional. As far as my own story goes, I could write a book on the parallels between my life and the movie *Dumb and Dumber*.

What I mean is, for many days of my life, I walked without the wisdom of God, as we all have at one time or another. I could tell you juicy stories from my Top 20 Hall of Fame of "dumb-and-dumber" decisions. For now, I'll give a few examples.

Dumb-and-dumber decision number one: In the movie, the main characters traded in their van for a scooter. It was an approximately three-thousand-dollar van which they exchanged for an almost four-hundred-dollar mini-scooter. Both characters ended up riding on the scooter as they traveled to Aspen, Colorado, during the middle of winter in freezing temperatures and with snow on the ground.

Well, I happen to really like motorcycles. (Can you see where this is going?) I had one of my own before I sold it, but there came a time when I really wanted my wife, Nancy, to have a motorcycle with me. So, what did I do?

Allow me to set the scene: Nancy was a nurse at the time and worked the night shift at a hospital, so she slept in the middle of the day. She drove the car that her dad had purchased for us before we got married. One day, while she was sleeping, I went out and sold her car, then took the money and bought brand new his-and-hers motorcycles! True story. Nancy ended up riding the motorcycle to work in freezing temperatures and, you guessed it, with snow on the ground! Needless to say, she was a real trooper, and we eventually sold her motorcycle.

Dumb-and-dumber decision number two: I used to chase success like the pot of gold at the end of a rainbow. For many years, I tirelessly worked day and night, seeking and searching for more power, fame, glory, and, of course, more money. I was the epitome of that famous line from the movie *Jerry Maguire*: "Show me the money!" The more money I got, the more I wanted. I was like a hamster in a running wheel, relentlessly chasing I'm not sure what. That was my life day after day, week after week.

Now, on the positive side, I know that money can do a lot of good things. But I finally realized (I believe, by the grace of God) that money is nothing but a *tool*. As simple as that sounds, it was a big-time revelation in my life. More than ever, I stepped into the freedom of never working for or serving money, but instead, making money work for *me*. What a big-time, wonderful revelation to fully comprehend that money is simply a tool, and I am not its servant. Thank You, Father God!

Dumb-and-dumber decision number three: I spent every weekend immersed in football, binge drinking, and overeating—big-time overeating! If I told you how much money I spent (and wasted) on all this, it would be completely embarrassing. Not only that, but the craziest part of it all is that I couldn't remember any of it because of my overindulgence in alcohol. Today, I am free from binge drinking, and I'm enjoying my weekends and all the football games so much better being 100 percent sober! Praise God. Now, I'm still working on the eating part, but I have made major progress. My personal health coach has me writing down my calorie intake every day. (Thank you, Mr. Smith.)

It's time to turn your dumb-and-dumber decisions into smart-and-smarter choices.

Life is a grind, and sometimes we have to make decisions that we don't want to make in order to become the person we want to be. One of the toughest decisions we have to make is to get out of bed in the morning when we're supposed to. Now, I would love to tell you that I get up every day, jump out of my bed, and twirl around in my bedroom just like Julie Andrews singing, "The hills are alive with the sound of music!" but that's just unrealistic. You'd think it would be easy to wake up and automatically be excited about the day. But all too often, we start selling ourselves on the idea that we don't *have* to wake up early, we don't *have* to discipline ourselves, or we don't *have* to do all the work ahead of us today.

I remember times when I was about to go on vacation. I wouldn't be able to sleep at night because I was so excited about the vacation. That's the way you should treat life. That's how you should treat every new day. Why? Because you know it's full of opportunity and full of the potential to create life and shape your destiny into one of greatness. But, your potential is limited to your ability to be disciplined when it comes to getting out of bed and accomplishing your tasks and goals for the day. The military is a great example of learning how to tell your *body* what to do instead of your body telling *you* what to do.

I'll tell you another story. One morning, an extremely wealthy man was looking out his window, which overlooked his magnificent estate, and he noticed one of his gardeners working in the orchard. He said to himself, "Wow, what I wouldn't give today to be that man working in the orchard and not have a problem or care in the world!" At the same time, the man in the orchard looked up and spotted the wealthy owner peering out of his window, and the gardener said to himself, "Wow, what I wouldn't give to be that wealthy man and have all his possessions!"

I have essentially lived the lives of both men. At times, I've had an extremely high net worth, and at other times, I've had almost nothing—with all the dumb-and-dumber stories to go along with those times. But, guess what? I finally learned an important lesson when a very wise man once told me, "No matter where you go, there you are." The moral of the story is simple. We can always look at someone else's life and think the grass is greener on the other side, but you are still living *your* life. Don't focus on living someone else's life. Instead, every single day and every single minute, focus on going to work on *yourself*—no matter who you are, where you are, or how far you've come in life. Each day, you must train your thought-life, your words, your emotions, and your will. Aligning your choices with the wisdom of God will produce a lifestyle of great habits.

Yes, I've been on the mountaintop, and I've been in the valley, as low as you can get. But no matter where I am, I'm still going to work on myself every single minute of every single day. That is why I have developed what I call the *11 Cornerstones* and the *8 Areas* over the course of many years of life experience. (More on these later.) With all my heart, I believe these tools of common sense were inspired by God. They are also a natural part of our everyday lives. They are decisions we have the freedom to make and which put the odds of excelling in our favor. I personally use them every single day to go to work on myself. I am convinced that they will make a difference in your life as well. Whenever I'm at home, in the marketplace, resting, grilling my favorite steak, or whenever I travel—whether it's for work, to follow the TCU Horned Frogs, or for leisure—I am consistently working on the *11 Cornerstones* and the *8 Areas* of my life.

The purpose of writing this book is to introduce these and many other principles to the world, all of which I have used in teaching, training, and coaching for many years. I have also used them in my real estate career as well as my contracting businesses. I firmly believe that the principles shared in *The Big*

Day have played a major role in helping to build quality leadership in one of the most successful contracting companies in Texas. The story is still being written. I could share powerful testimonies from dozens of great leaders to verify the accuracy of what I am saying. My desire is not to do that but to simply let the book speak for itself and let you be the judge and jury. I've said it countless times that there is no doubt in my mind — absolutely no doubt — that if you start practicing these concepts and ideas today, you will start to see a noticeable improvement in your life over the next few weeks and months.

Winners have their own personal mission statement.

My personal mission statement is this: Today, this big day, I will work on practicing to better myself in all *8 Areas* of my life by working with the *11 Cornerstones*, walking in the wisdom of God, being led by the Spirit of God, and developing my faith in both the natural and the spiritual realms of life.

Bottom line, I want my life to represent Matthew 5:16, which says, "Let your light shine before men in such a way that they may see your good deeds and moral excellence, and [recognize and honor and] glorify your Father who is in heaven."[2]

Your decision is the starting point.

Winning big starts with making the quality decision to be a warrior when it comes to working on yourself as an individual — not working on everyone else, but you. When? Today.

Success in life means winning big in every area.

In addition to your starting point, if you asked me how to describe winning big, I would say it's like a recipe with many quality ingredients or layers. When you're winning big, it means you're living a life of abundance filled with love, joy, peace, patience, integrity, humility, faith, kindness, mercy, forgiveness, self-control, good health, and financial stability, as well as uplifting and beneficial relationships. This abundance comes as a result of the practice of walking in God's wisdom, being led by the Spirit of God, and developing your faith.

Note that many of the above characteristics are fruit produced by the Spirit of God.[3] These are the ingredients to your recipe for winning big — both in the natural *and* in the spiritual realms, and, most importantly, in all *8 Areas* of your life! Having said this, I want to add one major point: stop living in the past and beating yourself up over poor choices you made yesterday, last week, last month, or last year. Winning big starts *today*. That's why today is *the big day*!

Keynotes:

- Your commitment to make a choice has power.
- Let this book serve as your personal coach.
- Our goal is to win big and turn away from a life of average or below average.
- Make the quality decision to be a warrior when it comes to working on yourself.
- Winning big is like a recipe consisting of many quality ingredients.
- Practice walking in God's wisdom.
- Practice being led by the Spirit of God.
- Practice developing your faith.
- See this day as a new day and the beginning of a new life; most importantly, don't beat yourself up over any poor choices you made in the past.
- **Today** is *the big day*!

CHAPTER TWO

One Step at a Time

"I am an atheist."

What if that's you? I want you to know that this book is still for you. I would love for this book to be your personal coach for success in every area of your life. Having spoken with and coached many individuals over the last few decades, I've often suggested that they read one of the thirty-one chapters of Proverbs (in the Bible) every day by reading the chapter number that corresponds with the number of the day of the month. Some have questioned me about the importance of reading Proverbs, so I will share several points I've shared with them:

1. There's more to life than what we know right now. It's hard to comprehend the expanse and complexities of the solar system, let alone everything else from A to Z. It's no surprise then that sometimes it's also hard to comprehend God and the universe.

2. Eternity is a lot longer than life on earth. So, just in case there is a God, and He is who He says He is, do you want to take the risk of not believing in Him and then living without Him forever?

3. Even if the books of the Bible were not written by the inspiration of the Holy Spirit, and if each one is just another fictional story—like books about the Easter Bunny, the Tooth Fairy, and Santa Claus—the Bible is still one of the greatest books ever written on business, let alone on life skills.

4. When you take the first step toward God, you will realize that He is a God who is all about relationship, and He wants to have a *personal* relationship with you, not a

religious relationship. God wants a one-on-one, spiritual relationship with you today. As you begin that relationship, you will see a real difference in the way your life is tracking. You will hear God in your subconscious and in your spirit as He engages with you in real conversations and even talks with you about the small things happening in your life.

5. God loves you just as you are today because of who He is, not because of who you are or are not.

Simply put, God is here to help us and not hurt us. In giving us His wisdom, He also assists us in making quality decisions so that we don't end up choosing a detrimental path for our lives.

If you're someone who feels hesitant about God, but you sense that He may be trying to speak to you, don't fight it—or Him. Just take it one step at a time, one day at a time, and begin forming a relationship with Him that you feel comfortable with right now.

"I am not a religious person, but I do believe in God."

In my interactions with people, this is a comment I have heard numerous times. This book could certainly seem religious in nature, but it's exactly the opposite. There's no life in religion; there's only life in relationship. *The Big Day* is a practical guide to support you in the natural *and* spiritual dimensions of life through a personal relationship with God. He gives us life and He gives us wisdom for life.

Designed to align you with that wisdom, what I have written is for every person who wants to be a champion in a *big* way: to be a leader, an entrepreneur, or a big success in whatever they do, setting a new standard of excellence for themselves and others. It is also written for anyone who intends to win big in life, from eliminating a destructive habit to breaking a record, from creating a high financial net worth to developing a cure for a disease. I could give thousands of examples, but whatever you're committed to, the good news is that you don't have to do it alone!

The day I decided not to be a self-made man, but a God-made man, my life changed for the best. Why? Because of a relationship. I chose not to do life on my own. I chose to think bigger than myself — and who is the biggest thinker of all time? It's God! People think God is small or boxed in, but that's only because their beliefs are small and boxed in. On the contrary, the Bible says that with God "all things are possible."[4]

So, here is your assignment: *ask God for help.* I literally mean right now. (Pause.) Now, take it one step at a time, and one day at a time. Again, let this book serve as your personal coach as you journey toward greater success in every area of life.

No matter who you are, God has a plan for you.

Contrary to popular belief, God is not mad at you or waiting to pass judgments of condemnation on you. He's not out in the cosmos somewhere with a big, Texas-sized flyswatter ready to slap you down at any moment. It doesn't matter what you've done in the past or even if you have trouble believing in God — He still wants you to know Him and the plan He has for your life.

Also, it doesn't matter whether you go to Sunday school or attend a church service every week. Whether you consider yourself a Methodist, Pentecostal, Catholic, Protestant, Muslim, Seventh-day Adventist, Mormon, Lutheran, atheist, Amish, American — black, white, yellow, or brown — or you're a part of the Church of Christ, Judaism, Scientology, Hinduism, a Chinese religion, the New Age, or any of the other hundreds of religions, it makes no difference. No matter who you are, what mistakes you've made, or if you're in prison right now, one thing remains true: God loves you *today* (your big day), and He has a wonderful plan for your life.

Did you catch that? *Today,* God has a wonderful plan for your life! He loves you whether you believe it or not. Written plainly, the Bible makes it clear that:

"Neither death nor life, nor angels nor principalities nor powers, nor things present nor things to come, nor height nor depth, nor any other created thing, shall be able to separate us from the love of God which is in Christ Jesus our Lord."[5]

God's love for you is *unconditional* today and every day. Wow, now that's the kind of relationship I want!

Ask yourself: Why not you?

You should say this to yourself every day from this point forward. Say it out loud so you can hear it with your own ears. As we just mentioned, with God all things are possible. He is willing to do the impossible for *anyone* to win big in life. So, why not you? Too many times we hear why it won't work and that we shouldn't get our hopes up. Others discourage us with words like, "Remember what happened last time?", or, "You're too _____ to do that!"

Nonsense! Get your hopes up! Be inspired and dream big! Start today! See and envision the impossible in your life—even right now. Why not you? It's *your* big day. *You* are made in God's image and likeness.[6] He wants to make you more than a conqueror,[7] the head and not the tail,[8] the victor not the victim.

No matter how you feel, what it looks like, what you've been through—your new day starts now! Again, why not you?! Stop asking for permission from others to be great. Your life is intended to be great, and not just someday or in the distant future. It can start today with the right perspective and alignments. You become what you think about the most. Think about greatness. Study the greatness of God and take time to meditate on it.

Yes, God wants to have a relationship with you today and every day, but perhaps the best news of all is that you don't have to figure out everything right now. Simply envision greatness for now and then take it one step at a time.

Keynotes:

- God loves you just as you are today because of who He is, not because of who you are or are not.
- God wants a one-on-one relationship with you whoever you are today.
- Build a relationship with God one step at a time.
- Shoot for the stars. Go for the gold. Be inspired.
- God's love for you is unconditional today and every day.
- God says, "All things are possible."[9]
- You are more than a conqueror.
- Begin to envision greatness in your life starting *today*.

CHAPTER THREE

The Natural and The Spiritual

Every area of your life has two forces working and operating simultaneously: the natural force and the spiritual force. Both forces are like gravity (a natural force), which operates invisibly. Both forces are also no respecter of persons. They affect all of us. The natural and the spiritual were never meant to be separated. In fact, life *is* 100 percent natural and 100 percent spiritual. They can operate independently but were designed to function *together* to achieve the maximum results of a successful life.

The natural force includes your will.

You have a free will when it comes to making choices. The natural consists of: what you reap when you sow, being in the right place at the right time, and, of course, your natural body and all its functions. It also includes all that you align yourself with, your written planning and goals, your Powerful Learning Agenda (more on this later), your disciplines, your attitudes, and your integrity (doing the small things right).

The spiritual force includes God's involvement.

This is made up of God's involvement in your life as well as your commitment to God, or, in other words, your relationship with Him made possible through the Son of God, Jesus Christ. You also have a role in the spiritual force. This includes receiving God's promises for your life, the daily practice of walking in the wisdom of God, being led by the Holy Spirit, and developing your most holy faith.[10]

The natural and the spiritual work hand in hand as two distinct realities that overlap one another. It's a natural, spiritual relationship. Your choices and what you do in the natural affect your spiritual life, and the effects of your relationship with God will flow into the natural side of your life. Each force influences the other.

Proverbs brings the natural and the spiritual together.

Read the following statements found in the book of Proverbs.[11] Here we see clear examples of the natural and the spiritual influencing one another and working together.

"Hear, O children, the instruction of a father, And pay attention [and be willing to learn] so that you may gain understanding and intelligent discernment" (Proverbs 4:1 AMP).

"Get [skillful and godly] wisdom! Acquire understanding [actively seek spiritual discernment, mature comprehension, and logical interpretation]!
Do not forget nor turn away from the words of my mouth.
Do not turn away from her (Wisdom) and she will guard and protect you;
Love her, and she will watch over you.
The beginning of wisdom is: Get [skillful and godly] wisdom [it is preeminent]!
And with all your acquiring, get understanding [actively seek spiritual discernment, mature comprehension, and logical interpretation]" (Proverbs 4:5-7 AMP).

"I have instructed you in the way of [skillful and godly] wisdom;
I have led you in upright paths.
When you walk, your steps will not be impeded [for your path will be clear and open];
And when you run, you will not stumble.
Take hold of instruction; [actively seek it, grip it firmly and] do not let go.
Guard her, for she is your life" (Proverbs 4:11-13 AMP).

"For they are life to those who find them,
And healing and health to all their flesh.

Watch over your heart with all diligence,
For from it flow the springs of life" (Proverbs 4:22–23 AMP).

"Let your eyes look directly ahead [toward the path of moral courage]
And let your gaze be fixed straight in front of you [toward the path of integrity].
Consider well and watch carefully the path of your feet,
And all your ways will be steadfast and sure.
Do not turn away to the right nor to the left [where evil may lurk];
Turn your foot from [the path of] evil" (Proverbs 4:25–26 AMP).

Your life consists of eight separate areas.

At this time, I want to introduce you to the *8 Areas* of your life. Note that they are not in any order of importance. Like the two forces of the natural and the spiritual, all eight areas are designed to work together as a whole.

Yes, there are seasons in your life when you will spend more time in one area than another, but never ignore any of the areas. If you do, it will handicap your highest calling. You can also operate in several areas at the same time. It's important to be aware of all the areas because by doing so, you can be intentional about improving each area so that none of them get left out.   = Balance

Comprehensive success in life is dependent on developing each of these eight areas:

1. Spiritual
2. School/Job/Career
3. Health
4. Financial
5. Hobbies
6. Rest
7. Powerful Learning Agenda (PLA)
8. Family/Friends

If you want to arrive at your destination, you have to know your starting point.

That statement may sound elementary, but it's foundational for identifying what you want in each of the *8 Areas* of your life. Take your health for example. Where are you regarding your health? Do you know, or do you know how to find out? Once you know, ask yourself if that's the condition (destination) in which you desire to stay. Would you like to improve? How? Once you know where you are and how you would like that to change, you'll have a realistic idea of the next best step to take.

There are three stages for the *8 Areas* of your life.

To make it simple, each area has three stages: the beginning, the intermediate, and the mature. In many cases, age has nothing to do with the stage in which you currently find yourself. For example, I know sixty-year-olds who are at the beginning stage of their finances. Why? Perhaps because of poor choices or poor circumstances. But whatever the reason, remember that none of us will get anywhere by beating ourselves up with condemnation or limiting ourselves to our circumstances. No matter what stage you're in, the starting point for progressing further is today. *The big day* means it's a new day.

 God is not just in "first place"; He is in all places.

For all my life, I've grown up listening to many well-meaning teachers and leaders reiterating the following principle: "Put God in first place. Your family second. And your job third." Now, I know that sounds practical, and the idea of that statement may give you a warm feeling inside, but it's far from accurate. God is in *all* places — in the beginning, in the end, and everywhere in between. He's the Alpha and Omega,[12] the First and the Last. He wants to be as involved in your relationships with family members as He is in your career, as He is in your hobbies, and as He is in your relationship with Him! The more equal His involvement in all of these, the greater the success you will experience in each of them.

God wants to be involved in all *8 Areas* of your life.

One of God's attributes is being omnipresent (in all places simultaneously). As much as He's omnipresent, He cares about your life. This means that He cares to be involved in every stage of every area of your life. As Psalm 139 describes, He knows when you sit and when you get up, and He's acquainted with all your ways, including all your thoughts before you even think them.[13]

Not only is He intricately acquainted with you, and not only does He care about you, but He also has a wonderful plan for all *8 Areas* of your life. He loves you and wants to lead you into these plans in each of these areas. This can include small and/or large decisions or circumstances. It's the wisdom of God to integrate the spiritual and the natural because they were meant to fully function together. Bringing Him into every area of your life isn't "super spiritual" but rather very practical.

Combine the natural and the spiritual within the storms of life.

I wrote the following letter to myself on April 24, 2017, in remembrance of my grandson, Justin Whipple. I love you, Justin.

> When the storms of life assault you, how do you cope with the pain, grief, confusion, and all the unanswered questions? Do you blame yourself or others? Do you allow all the negative and destructive human emotions to overtake you? No, this is how you cope:
>
> First, realize that life has two sides: the natural and the spiritual. Add the spiritual to your natural and you will get supernatural strength and peace in the midst of the storm.
>
> Next, don't play "God" by trying to figure everything out. We were never meant to live life as self-made men and women. Life itself, without the spiritual, is extremely empty and shallow and will only produce

dead-ends. Even your natural human body doesn't last forever. However, God loves you and has a wonderful plan for your life, a plan that includes your spirit living forever. Embrace the relationship of the spiritual. Jesus has made a way for each of us. All you have to do is receive it. Even in the midst of a great tragedy, you can experience your greatest hour. This doesn't happen by human strength but simply by allowing God's peace to step inside you. The Bible refers to this as "the peace of God, which surpasses all understanding."[14] It is very powerful.

Listed below are several methods I have used not to succumb to defeat during the storms:

- Draw near to God through the Scriptures. Meditate upon them throughout the day and into the night. (Here's a note on retraining your thinking: if you can't sleep, that is the best time to read your Bible or at least pray.)
- Get professional, godly counseling.
- Don't try to connect all the dots or answer all the unanswered questions in your own reasoning.
- Surround yourself with team members who are praying for you and encouraging you. I am so thankful for my team members.
- Stay focused on being grateful for the thousands of blessings, literally, that God has brought into your life. Remind yourself of these blessings over and over throughout the day.
- Stay plugged in by serving people, serving your team, and getting your mind off yourself.
- Get up, get dressed, clean yourself up, wash your face, fix your hair, put on your best clothes, and top it off with your favorite cologne. (Women: put your makeup on as well, and wear your favorite perfume.)
- Take one day at a time.

- Go to the gym, go for a jog, or take a long walk outside.
- Speak words of life over yourself, your team, and your family.
- Decide to never ever, ever take your family or teammates for granted.

Life is at its best when you combine the natural and the spiritual.

Writing this letter is not an attempt to remain positive. It's a realistic view of life when everything is upside-down and when you're going through the toughest times. When you separate the natural from the spiritual, you're basically on your own. That is not God's best for your life. Whether you're on the mountaintop or in the midst of a storm, life is at its best when you're operating in *both* dimensions: 100 percent in the spiritual and 100 percent in the natural.

Keynotes:

- The two forces working and operating simultaneously are the natural force and the spiritual force.
- They were designed to fully function together to achieve maximum results.
- You have *8 Areas* of your life. You are also designed to operate in several areas at the same time.
- There are three stages for each of the *8 Areas* of your life: the beginning, the intermediate, and the mature.
- God wants to be involved in all *8 Areas* of your life, including all the small and large decisions or circumstances.
- Whether you're on the mountaintop or in the midst of a storm, life is at its best when you're operating in *both* dimensions: 100 percent in the spiritual and 100 percent in the natural.

CHAPTER FOUR

Wisdom and Discipline

The Spirit of Wisdom is a part of the nature of God. Practice aligning yourself with the wisdom of God using intelligent discernment in every decision you make concerning all *8 Areas* of your life. A few of the major ways to gain wisdom include asking God for it, reading the Bible, and speaking wisdom over yourself throughout the day. Align what you do, the people with whom you associate, and the choices you make with the wisdom of God. Even when you feel as dumb as a post or when you're just not sure which direction to take, start declaring over yourself, "I have the wisdom of God in every choice I make and in every direction I take."

Wisdom is not automatic. Wisdom does not just fall on you. It's something you go and get. The Bible says to "get wisdom."[15] That means it's available for all of us. That is why you can *practice* getting the wisdom of God every single day. You don't take a day off from acquiring God's wisdom. You don't take a day off from God. Every step you take throughout the day — no matter how small or how practical — should be aligned with God's wisdom.

Isn't it interesting that when things are going great in your life, you stop doing the basics? You tend to get lazy in both the natural and spiritual dimensions of life. You start living on yesterday's anointing or yesterday's success. You justify why you make lazy or dumb choices.

One example is with your physical exercise. You really don't know what shape you're in until you put a demand on your body. This analogy relates to both the natural and the spiritual. That's why it's important to be in good shape physically, mentally, and spiritually. All three of these areas should be aligned with the wisdom of God. Better yet, all *8 Areas* of your life should be aligned with the wisdom of God. When you consistently align your decisions and your life with the wisdom of God over several weeks, you'll see a noticeable difference. This is something that takes practice every single day.

Spiritually, physically, and mentally utilizing the wisdom of God with determination will build up your stamina and endurance to run a great race. The wisdom of God will produce so many good qualities in your life. One main quality it will produce for you in the natural force is discipline. Wow! So, it's going to take the wisdom of God *along with discipline* to run your race. A good example of this is found in the apostle Paul's first letter to the Corinthian church as he describes how to win your race and discipline your body.[16] The self-control and wisdom spoken of in that passage are for all *8 Areas* of your life.

What does this look like practically? The following checklist describes the fruit of a wise individual. Developing wisdom and its fruit in your life takes practice every day. Meditating on these qualities of wisdom and daily practicing them will help you reach maximum effectiveness in all *8 Areas* of your life!

WISDOM CHECKLIST

- ✓ Every day, throughout the day, practice walking in the wisdom of God and being led by the Spirit of God.
- ✓ Study and meditate on the Word of God several times a day.
- ✓ Be calm and peaceful in your day-to-day activities.
- ✓ Be extremely disciplined spiritually, mentally, and physically, and always improve in these with a ferocious Powerful Learning Agenda (PLA).
- ✓ Practice developing your faith daily.
- ✓ Have a great exercise regimen, including two cardio and two core exercises per week.
- ✓ Never move forward with a decision based only on how good something looks.
- ✓ Don't focus on or be consumed by things over which you have no control, especially people.
- ✓ Follow effective time-management principles with a plan for all *8 Areas* of your life.
- ✓ Have great systems and written goals for all *8 Areas* of your life.
- ✓ Practice implementing wisdom in your speech; be careful about what you say.
- ✓ See yourself as a wise person making wise and prudent choices.
- ✓ Sow a minimum of 10 percent of your finances into great works.
- ✓ Understand that the beginning is the most important part of any endeavor. Spend the amount of time that is necessary for proper preparation.
- ✓ Focus on today with an understanding of the future.
- ✓ Align yourself with great people and groups.
- ✓ When you face a problem, call it an opportunity and handle it with calmness and peace.
- ✓ Instead of being easily offended, upset, or lashing out at people, be patient and open to understanding others.
- ✓ Be a kind individual to all people.
- ✓ Be careful of what you consume in your body.

- ✓ Never base decisions on following the crowd.
- ✓ Be grateful for what you've been given.
- ✓ Don't try to figure everything out in your own strength.
- ✓ Challenge your team and other people to be their best.
- ✓ Ensure your level of integrity is second to none.
- ✓ Always take the initiative.
- ✓ Have a great work ethic for all *8 Areas* of your life.
- ✓ Be accountable and hold your team accountable.
- ✓ Understand that money is simply a tool.
- ✓ See the best in people; refuse to be critical.
- ✓ Be a skilled, top producer in all that you do. Be way above average.

Keynotes:

- Practice aligning yourself with the wisdom of God in every decision you make concerning each of the *8 Areas* of your life.
- Practice building your stamina to be in good shape physically, mentally, and spiritually.
- The wisdom of God will produce many beneficial qualities in your life.
- Read the Wisdom Checklist out loud weekly.

CHAPTER FIVE

The Danger of Living Without Wisdom

In the previous chapter, we discussed wisdom and how it produces the fundamental fruit of discipline. Let's talk a bit about the fundamental fruit produced from the tree of foolishness, which lacks wisdom. In other words, what outward fruit do we find manifesting in our behavior when we're not aligned with wisdom? Listed below is my Hall of Fame of foolish manifestations. But before you read these, I want to make the point that I demonstrated these manifestations on a regular basis in my past — all of them!

- Chasing money, security, fame, or a title
- Worrying (which means you see yourself as your own god)
- Being lazy or slothful; having a low degree of self-discipline
- Being out of shape physically, mentally, or spiritually
- Being easily offended
- Having an over-the-top judgmental attitude (having no patience for others and their weaknesses)
- Feeling sorry for yourself; self-pity
- Having a sense of entitlement (e.g., "Don't you realize who I am?")
- Having a self-made man/woman attitude (the focus is on me)
- Being hot-tempered, rude, or easily irritated
- Consuming the wrong things (e.g., drugs)
- Not thinking before speaking; being argumentative; causing strife in relationships
- Making unwise choices; having alignments with the wrong people or the wrong situations; watching destructive television shows; visiting poisonous websites

- Having no plans or goals; being "loosey-goosey" or careless
- Being motivated by retirement, e.g., "I can't wait until I can just relax / enjoy life / play golf / finally live the good life / sleep in / take it easy / do whatever I want, whenever I want."
- Trying to figure everything out that concerns tomorrow or the future
- Always being in a hurry or placing too much importance on adhering to a schedule
- Feeling an urgency to say everything you know; feeling you have so much to say and so little time to say it; being quick to speak and slow to listen

This list should not cause you or anyone else to feel condemned. It's simply a practical means of awakening your mental faculties and helping you see your behaviors objectively. That way, you have an idea of where to start reevaluating the choices you make every day.

All of these characteristics share one commonality: your focus in life is all about *yourself* and how *self-important* you are. Narcissism is one of the top tools the devil uses against human beings to trap them in a life of turmoil and stress. The other form of narcissism is false humility. Both motivate you to do "whatever it takes," and while that sounds motivational and even faith-filled, it's the opposite. You're viewing yourself as the god of your life, doing "whatever it takes" for your own good, to promote yourself and/or maintain the appearance of having it all together.

To keep your life in the proper perspective, one of your core assignments on earth is to "lay down"17 your life for the sake of others, which takes the focus off you and places it onto giving. Valuing others will take your life further than you can imagine, and the reward is always worth it. That said, there is a balance in focusing on yourself for the sake of retraining your paradigms.

Bottom line: start practicing your alignment with wisdom instead! Starting today, choose to make wise decisions in *all 8 Areas* of your life. I love this concept!

Keynotes:

- Living without wisdom is dangerous for you and others.
- A self-focused mentality motivates you to do "whatever it takes" for your own good.
- Narcissism and false humility are traps.
- Awaken your mental faculties to keep you from making unwise choices.
- Unwise choices produce turmoil and stress.

CHAPTER SIX

Building a Keynote Book

I love to watch people. Over many years, I have observed that a small (and I mean *small*) percentage of a church audience will take notes during the message. The same goes for training seminars. Without taking notes, what are the odds that those participants will remember what they heard a week later, or a month later, let alone a year later? Most likely, they won't.

Instead of just sitting there, taking great notes gives you the opportunity to go back to them, and, better yet, it causes your productivity to skyrocket. It's common sense that people remember significantly less over the days, weeks, and especially months that pass. What should we do about this?

The answer is simple: start taking notes *today*! And when you do, be wise in the way you do it. Another small detail (and by small, I mean gigantic): a high percentage of those who make an effort to take notes do not have a strategy for organizing and archiving those notes.

This changes today.

Obviously, the purpose of taking notes and reviewing them over and over is to train yourself to do what is necessary to win big. This training is an important ingredient of a great life. Greatness is God's will for your life, but it does not always just fall on you. In other words, God is moving on your behalf and has a wonderful plan for your life, but He puts the ball in your court when it comes to choices and commitment. Greatness requires action on your part — every single day.

The amazing thing is that it's not so hard to do. You're not being required to climb the tallest mountain or swim the deepest river. It's simply a matter of developing some discipline to get started. With that said, I would like to introduce you to the term *keynote* and the system of keynoting. Making a note of anything that stands out to you, inspires you, teaches you, or moves you forward is what I define as a keynote.

The system of keynoting adds structure for the big day.

Building a *Keynote Book* is step one for retraining your thinking. The purpose of a system of keynoting is to record, organize, and maintain all the things (i.e., thoughts, attitudes, disciplines, etc.) that you want to grow in and reinforce in your life. Keynoting will produce greatness in your ability to train and prepare yourself for *the big day*, which is *today*.

- Start with a three-ring binder for the year and label it *Keynotes*.
- Make a new three-ring binder for each year from this point forward.
- Have eight different sections within the binder for the *8 Areas* of your life as mentioned in chapter 3.

Yes, instead of using a three-ring binder, you can also create your keynote system using a computer or other electronic device. It doesn't matter which form you choose; the important part is that you have an organized system for taking notes everywhere you go no matter where you are, what time it is, or what the occasion may be. Then, place the keynotes you make into the respective folder for that area of your life. (If you do make a three-ring binder, be sure to use reinforced three-ring paper.)

The best way of taking notes (keynoting) calls for a few important reminders:

1) You don't need to write down everything you hear.

2) Write down only what inspires you.

3) Write down only the facts and figures you want to remember.

Changing your thinking changes your life.

Your life will completely change when you allow God to change your thinking. The only way to change your thought patterns is to change your paradigms and perspectives. That is why the system of keynoting is so powerful. In effect, it detoxes your brain from the junk you have believed and the way this junk has trained you to think. We will discuss more about this critical topic throughout the book.

Growing proficiently and powerfully will require a strong dose of PLA.

If you ask me which of the *8 Areas* of your life is the most important, my answer may shock you. Each area is important, but I believe there are two areas that are most vital to your growth: your thinking (thus, the PLA) and your spiritual life.

Aligning your thinking with the wisdom of God will cause your life as you know it to grow and flourish so that "you may prosper in all things and be in health, just as your soul prospers."[18] Retraining your thinking allows you to prosper. With that said, it's critical that you develop a Powerful Learning Agenda (PLA) for all *8 Areas* of your life, the purpose of which is to help you retrain your thinking. (See *Chapter Sixteen: Cornerstone 3 – Your Thinking* for more details.)

Make keynotes for all *8 Areas* in order to develop your PLA list. (You'll see why keynoting as you go is critically important.) If you're at the beginning stage of any of the *8 Areas* of your life, you're like a patient in critical condition being wheeled on a gurney into the emergency room of life, needing the transfusion of a great PLA with the wisdom of God. Growing in any area of your life requires a plan for how and what you will specifically invest into so you may develop that area.

My top ten PLA list for all *8 Areas* of my life includes:

- The Bible
- God / the wisdom of God
- My wife (my second-best friend after God)

47

- Great books from great leaders
- Autobiographies
- Magazine articles
- Church services; training seminars
- Mentors
- Great and clean comedians
- My personal trainer

I have many more, but these are just a few.

Use your keynotes effectively.

Again, when you make a keynote, each one will correspond to one of the *8 Areas* of your life. Starting now, and at the beginning of each year, organize these notes and put them into the appropriate categories:

1. Keynotes for going to work on myself
2. Keynotes for going to work on my wealth plan
3. Keynotes for going to work on my career, formal education, or the starting of a company
4. Keynotes for going to work on my health plan
5. Keynotes for going to work on my hobbies
6. Keynotes for going to work on my relationships with family and friends
7. Keynotes for going to work on my spiritual plan
8. Keynotes for going to work on my rest plan

Note that some areas will overlap with other areas. Also, include keynotes for your living will and testament.

Here comes the fun part.

Block out ninety minutes in your schedule. Take out the keynote pages which you just created for each one of the *8 Areas*. You should have eight separate documents. Write down what you desire to accomplish in your life in each area. You will have two categories: short-term, between now and the next twelve months, and long-term, twelve months from now and after.

Don't make your points too detailed. Also, avoid the temptation to figure everything out about your life and be careful not to over-spiritualize your goals. Take a deep breath and simply write down one to three things you might like to accomplish in each of the *8 Areas*. Try not to outthink yourself, or, as they say in football, "out-punt your coverage." Just relax and have fun!

The good news is, this process is a great tool to show you what you're generally, or even subconsciously, thinking about. Wow! I legitimately believe this is a great concept. Most people aren't trying to get to the bottom of what they are thinking about, but knowing what you're thinking about positions you on the offense of life. In fact, once you complete this process, you are already in the upper minority of all human beings. You already have an advantage! We will discuss this more throughout the book.

Dedicate time for keynoting.

Each calendar quarter, set a dedicated appointment for yourself to spend approximately two hours to carefully read and meditate on all the keynotes you made for each of the *8 Areas*.

Typically, on New Year's Day, or within a few days thereafter, I spend approximately five hours reading my keynotes from the previous year. I then categorize my top twenty-five keynotes according to the *8 Areas* of my life.

Just imagine, years from now, sharing your keynotes with your grandchildren and setting an example of greatness in their lives. Or imagine generations down the road, when perhaps your grandchildren's grandchildren find those notes and pick them up. At that moment, you become alive, sowing greatness into their lives. Imagine the impact you could make in someone's life! That's my number one priority in writing this book.

The high calling you and I have is bigger than us. One more time: our high calling should be *bigger* than who we are.

Our calling is to be everything—and I mean everything—that God had in mind when He created us. We are designed to leave a legacy of His greatness.

Your collection of keynotes eventually becomes a testimony of your life, or your life's book. The volumes of notes over many years make up that book. I can only imagine how nice and how powerful it would have been to receive keynote books from my dad's dad's dad. That's bigger than life. Wow! Start this today! Teach this to your family and your friends. Better yet, give them a copy of *The Big Day* so they can read all about it.

If you are ready to create an above-and-beyond PLA, then I highly recommend the following books, biographies, and magazines.

Some of my top books:

- *Angels* by Billy Graham
- *As a Man Thinketh* by James Allen
- *Awaken the Giant Within: How to Take Immediate Control of Your Mental, Emotional, Physical and Financial Destiny!* by Anthony Robbins
- *Battlefield of the Mind: Winning the Battle in Your Mind* by Joyce Meyer
- *Becoming a Better You: 7 Keys to Improving Your Life Every Day* by Joel Osteen
- *Developing the Leader Within You* by John C. Maxwell
- *Don't Sweat the Small Stuff . . . and It's All Small Stuff* by Richard Carlson
- *How to Win Friends & Influence People* by Dale Carnegie
- *Living Beyond Your Feelings: Controlling Emotions So They Don't Control You* by Joyce Meyer
- *Man's Search for Meaning* by Viktor E. Frankl
- *Over the Top: Moving from Survival to Stability, from Stability to Success, from Success to Significance* by Zig Ziglar
- *Psycho-Cybernetics* by Maxwell Maltz
- *See You at the Top* by Zig Ziglar

- *Start Strong, Finish Strong* by Dr. Kenneth H. Cooper and Dr. Tyler C. Cooper
- *The E-Myth Revisited: Why Most Small Businesses Don't Work and What to Do About It* by Michael Gerber
- The Holy Bible
- *The Magic of Thinking Big* by David J. Schwartz
- *The Millionaire Next Door: The Surprising Secrets of America's Wealthy* by Thomas J. Stanley and William D. Danko
- *The Power of Positive Thinking* by Dr. Norman Vincent Peale
- *The Richest Man in Babylon* by George S. Clason
- *The Shack* by William P. Young
- *The Total Money Makeover: A Proven Plan for Financial Fitness* by Dave Ramsey
- *Thinking for a Change: 11 Ways Highly Successful People Approach Life and Work* by John C. Maxwell

Some of my top biographies, which may be found on the Biography Channel[19] or YouTube:

- Abraham Lincoln
- Amelia Earhart
- Andrew Carnegie
- Anne Frank
- Barack Obama
- Benjamin Franklin
- Bill Gates
- Billy Graham
- Charles Lindbergh
- Conrad Hilton
- Donald Trump
- Albert Einstein
- Henry Ford
- Indra Nooyi
- Jesse Owens
- John D. Rockefeller

- John Kennedy
- Martin Luther King
- Mary Kay Ash
- Mother Theresa
- Oprah Winfrey
- Sam Walton
- *The Presidents of the United States*, Episode 1
- Thomas Jefferson
- Tiger Woods
- Tim Tebow
- Walt Disney
- Warren Buffett
- Winston Churchill

Some of my top magazines:

- *Entrepreneur*
- *Fast Company*
- *Flying*
- *Forbes*
- *Guideposts*
- *Harvard Business Review*
- *Inc.*
- *Men's Health*
- *Reader's Digest*
- *Sports Illustrated*
- *Success*
- *The Good Life*

Hopefully, these lists give you an idea of how to be aggressive and proactive with your PLA.

Build a keynote system along with a PLA.

A keynote system will help you organize and remind yourself of the great discoveries, principles, truth, and wisdom you have come across in your life. The system is for all *8 Areas* of your life and should allow you to take notes everywhere you go.

Your PLA will help you change your thinking (and your alignments), therefore detoxing you from all the junk in your brain. The Bible is a great start for your PLA. Read it daily.

Plan dedicated appointments to review your keynotes.

At the end of each calendar quarter, spend approximately two hours in a dedicated appointment reading and meditating on your keynotes for that quarter. Each year, spend approximately a day and a half categorizing your top twenty-five notes of the year into the *8 Areas* of your life.

Remember, you're writing a book about your life to leave to family, friends, and even humankind. This is part of your legacy. Never underestimate the testimony of greatness in *your* life.

Keynotes:

- Make a keynote for anything you hear that stands out to you and may help you.
- Create a system for organizing and maintaining all your keynotes.
- Think about what you're thinking about.
- Changing your thinking changes your life.
- Block out ninety minutes and write down (in your Keynote Book) what you would like to achieve, writing one to three items for each of the *8 Areas* of your life.
- Set dedicated appointments for reviewing your keynotes and PLA.
- Develop your skill sets and skill proficiency.
- Readers are leaders.
- Build up your home library.
- Keynoting essentially becomes a testimony of your life and a legacy to leave to future generations.

CHAPTER SEVEN

Living in the Right Time Zone: Part 1

What will you do with today? Isn't that a great question to ask yourself!

Seriously, ask yourself what you're going to do with your day today. After all, *today* is your *big day*! Do you firmly believe that? Here's another question: Does it mean yesterday, or even tomorrow, is your big day too? No, it doesn't! Let's look at the facts.

Your yesterday ended yesterday. It's over. It's done with. It's literally history. And unless you've been given a promise from God about tomorrow, then tomorrow has no guarantees. You may have expectations and plans, but things usually turn out differently than expected anyway. Bottom line: that's why today is your big day. It's a mind-set, an attitude of being properly focused and aligned so that you're not living your life out of three separate "time zones." Your focus is today. It makes a lot of sense. Living your life dependent on the other two time zones can be extremely nonproductive and detrimental to your success in any (and every) area of life.

For example, how much time do we spend on living in the past? We study the past; we rehearse the past; and sometimes we torture ourselves with the past. We say things like, "If only I could or would have," or, "I should have . . . ." What makes it even worse is when we hook our past up to today, like a vehicle pulling a trailer. Everything in the trailer represents the past: all our past mistakes, all our dumb decisions, all our unproductive relationships. But this ends up allowing our past to shape our day today. If you let it, the past can harass you like a big bully every single day. The bully of the past shouts and screams at you, convincing you to believe:

- It's too late.

- I'm too old.
- I've made too many mistakes.
- That person or thing hurt me too much.
- It wasn't fair.
- It's not my fault.
- It was my fault.
- I tried that and look at what happened.
- I failed miserably.
- I lost everything.
- I'm just a born loser.
- They must be right.
- Unforgiveness is OK.
- They burned me.
- I was salesman of the year, after all.
- I was born that way.
- It was the recession.
- My credit score is horrible.
- My coach or my teacher told me I was just average.
- I was never very smart in school.
- I've been tested and diagnosed with ADD.
- I'm not a good speller.
- I don't understand those computers.
- I always have a hard time taking tests.

Some of those things might be true or partially true, but no matter the context, none of those statements can ultimately shape who you are or define you as an individual. After all, you're made in God's image.[20] It's His perspective of you that defines you.

However, when we try to forget our past by medicating ourselves with drugs, alcohol, excess food, wrong people, wrong types of relationships, and/or entertainment (like sports, TV, etc.), we convince ourselves that *that's* who we are. Nothing could be further from the truth. We let our wrong (inferior) behavior dictate our destiny, basing it on outward, temporary actions instead of our eternal, spiritual inheritance. (Wisdom, for example, is our inheritance in God.)

What you believe determines your reality. If the negative fruit listed above describes your reality, practice changing what you believe! Especially change what you believe about yourself, God, and others. Remember, *today* is your big day to change!

Most of us have been trained to believe that we can learn from the past. In my opinion, there's about 5 percent truth to that and about 95 percent garbage. We learn and grow by forward thinking. You don't win in reverse. You never win on defense; you win on offense. I'm not saying we should totally disregard the past, but instead, we shouldn't use it as our personal trainer for how to live today.

By telling us what we can or can't do, the past limits our thinking and our paradigm of what it means to win big *today*. Thus, it ends up training us to believe in "average" or "below average" and gradually lowers our expectations, our hopes, and our dreams. It becomes an oppressive dictator, and we end up victims of each day instead of victors. Without the proper perspective, our past can beat us up and suck the life right out of us.

Another reason this happens is the simple fact that an enemy exists. We call him Satan or the Accuser, and he's not just anyone's enemy. Due to his corrupt nature, he is actually everyone's enemy. What does this mean for us?

Satan has three primary goals for our lives: to *steal*, to *kill*, and to *destroy*.[21] Not only that, but he doesn't come in and say, "Good morning! I'm here to steal, kill, and destroy your life today by getting you to focus on your past!" On the contrary, he subtly gets you thinking about the past. Using guilt and shame, he manages to harass and intimidate you until you become your own worst enemy with all the accusation and condemnation that you place upon yourself.

It's a vicious downward spiral that's almost impossible to break if we keep living in the past. We end up defeating ourselves with the wrong mind-set, believing that the past is here to help us. Again, nothing could be further from the truth.

How are you being trained?

We are well-trained with clichés that sound good, like "We can all learn from our past," or, "I'm not going to make that mistake again." But then we end up making that mistake again and letting the recurrences increasingly define us. The media also deems you a loser when you lose the big game, using words like "devastating loss." Often, this develops negative self-programming within you, leading you to believe that the past defines who you are.

But wait! Great, great news! Read all about it! Shout it from the rooftops! Your past does *not* need to define who you are.

Practice dropping the past every day, starting today. Even now, drop it and let it fall to the ground like a lead balloon. Don't rehearse it; don't meditate on it; don't replay it over and over in your mind. Don't limit yourself to yesterday's successes or failures. Don't let the unredeemed opinions of others define who you are. Don't let a test that you take tell you what you would be best at doing. (Hogwash!) Let God define your past, your future, and who you are!

The Bible offers great advice about how to treat others. Use it as a guide of wisdom in how to treat yourself too. It says, "Hate what is wrong. Hold tightly to what is good."[22] When we "drop the past," we make the choice to hate what is wrong and what prevents us from living an average life; instead, we choose to cling to what is good and moves us onward to winning big.

Dropping your past will move you forward.

From this point, it's time to take the next big step. For the next seventy-five to ninety days, practice training your habits.

Starting today, the first and most important step for you to take is that of training yourself to drop the past. I give you my word of honor that after consistently training yourself to drop the past, you will see things differently in every area of your life. You'll begin to recognize the greatness that you carry within you. Practicing this will transform you more than you could ever imagine. You will begin to see the chains and shackles fall off, releasing you into the abundant life that God intended you to live. Note that this takes training every day, throughout the day. In fact, as often as your past harasses you, you must stand against it like a warrior. Absolutely forget the limitations of yesterday.

The apostle Paul, who wrote two-thirds of the New Testament, said it like this: "Brethren, I do not regard myself as having laid hold of it yet; but one thing I do: forgetting what lies behind and reaching forward to what lies ahead."[23] Did you get that? It's worth repeating again and again. Forget what lies behind! One more time: forget what lies behind! Just saying that releases me from the bondage of the past. My future is today. Hallelujah! Is that good news or what? Truly, *today is your big day*.

Use wisdom in letting the past help you.

Let's continue discussing how to use the wisdom of God to articulate and identify what we *should* remember about the past. In other words, instead of being hindered by our past, how can we make the most of it? To make it simple, I have put together a checklist at the end of this chapter called "Wisdom's Checklist of the Past," which has some ideas of how we can use the past to make our *big day* the best it can be.

It reminds me of David, a king of Israel long ago. Many of us know the story of David and Goliath. When David went up against the giant, Goliath, David brought to his own remembrance the victories of God in his life, explaining that he "killed both the lion and the bear; and this uncircumcised Philistine will be like one of them, since he has taunted and defied the armies of the living God."[24] David applied wisdom to his past, which gave him the strength and confidence to defeat the giant. Not only that, but agreeing with wisdom opened the door for the miraculous. He experienced the spiritual fully operating with the natural. Talk about winning *big*!

Learn how to catapult your future into greatness.

What is it that we *can* take from our past and align with the wisdom of God which will launch us into the greatness He intended for us to experience? What choices can we make today, or what choices have we *already* made, that will set us up for this greatness? Here's a checklist of days, decisions, events, etc. from the past we can bring into our day today to keep us in alignment with the wisdom of God.

WISDOM'S CHECKLIST OF THE PAST

- ✓ The date you committed or recommitted your life to Christ
- ✓ Days and "marker moments" when you decided to make a positive change to improve your life
- ✓ Special holidays or events with loved ones
- ✓ Taking the bad decisions that you made and turning that negative situation into a great opportunity to catapult you to greatness
- ✓ Past movies and television shows that are classics.
- ✓ Special pictures of events and loved ones
- ✓ Learning how to keep from making the same mistake over and over
- ✓ Having a track record of taking care of your health
- ✓ Being able to laugh at yourself with all the funny things you've done, e.g., disco dancing, wearing leisure suits, or owning shag carpet
- ✓ Believing that anything is possible with God
- ✓ Honoring the sacrifice of people who lay down their lives for our freedom; this includes policemen, firefighters, the military, etc.
- ✓ Great events that have shaped America or the world
- ✓ Great revivals and spiritual awakenings in the past
- ✓ Not allowing yourself to get caught up in the drama of others and their pasts
- ✓ Making the choice (as often as necessary) to agree with words of life over yourself instead of engaging in negative self-talk
- ✓ Refusing to dwell on the past
- ✓ Reading great books and biographies written by coaches, leaders, revivalists, etc. whose lives were touched by God and who influenced many others
- ✓ Spending time studying and meditating on the Holy Bible, inspired by the words of God, teaching all human beings how to live great (abundant) lives today

Keynotes:

- What you do with today determines your tomorrow.
- One of the negative time zones is focusing on yesterday.
- We spend too much time living in the past.
- Your past tends to harass you like a big bully.
- Today is your big day.
- Our past trains us to live an average or below average life.
- Satan has three goals for your life: to steal, kill, and destroy it.
- Satan will use your past to accuse you of being a failure. Nothing could be further from the truth.
- For the next seventy-five to ninety days, practice training your habits to stop dwelling on the past; instead, align yourself with the wisdom of God.
- Paul said to "forget what lies behind."
- Use wisdom to identify what you should remember from your past.

CHAPTER EIGHT

Living in the Right Time Zone: Part 2

If we intend to succeed in every area of our lives today, we can't limit ourselves to the time zone of our past. But what's the other wrong time zone that we often get caught up in? The time zone of the future. Something we all need to work on is not being overly focused on tomorrow. Doing so proves to be unproductive and often detrimental to winning big as we become distracted and lose sight of how important today is — and that *today* is *the big day*.

Live in *today* while being excited about the future.

Being excited about the future is one thing. We all have those special events in our lives that we look forward to, like your dream vacation, closing on the new house, the big game, finally getting the right job, or your wedding day. Sometimes it's the big break you've been waiting for or closing that big business deal after months and months of hard work.

No doubt those events are special to us. The question is, what are we doing about *today* while we wait for these events to happen? Are we losing our focus on the importance of today? Are we making the most out of today? Are we living consistently with our goals today, or are we so attached to what's ahead of us that we neglect to stop and do the small things right today? Right now is important. This moment means something — if you let it. Don't let the future keep you from seizing the day today. Bottom line: live in the right time zone!

Don't dread your future.

Distracted by what might or could happen, we allow the future to rob the potential from today. Just as looking forward to the future can cause us to lose focus, so too (and even more so) does the constant harassing of dread and worry shift our focus from winning big today. We dread or worry about the weather, the coming storm, the economy, the election, having to get up early, the procedure that's going to be done, the MRI, the doctor's report, getting too old to find Mr. or Mrs. Right, the lawsuit, the 401(k), losing money in the stock market, and then the granddaddy of them all: "What if . . . ?" Without proper training of our thoughts and emotions, we anticipate failure like there is a reward for it because we're so trained to focus on catastrophes or failures that *might* happen.

Yes, it's good to think ahead and prepare for situations, but I'm talking about getting caught up in the fear of failure or the worry and dread of future concerns. Preparation is wisdom. Losing focus on what's important today steals the potential of *the big day*.

But to make it worse, we sometimes dread *the worst*. For example, fearing the worst-case scenario when your loved one gets on that motorcycle. Or even fearing death itself, whether it happens to you or someone you love. This concern is especially distracting if you feel you've made so many mistakes that you'd probably go to hell if you die. Dreading eternity will certainly cause you to lose your focus on today!

The truth is, God made a way for you to receive what you don't deserve—it's a gift of salvation made available to you because of the greatness of His love for you, and all you have to do is believe Him and receive Him. Simple! God loves you and has a wonderful plan for your life *today*!

Freedom is for the big day.

The writer of the book of Hebrews describes the One who conquered fear and death, *and* the fear of death! This gives us the opportunity and the confidence to live with hope for *the big day* today.

> "Since the children have flesh and blood, he [Jesus] too shared in their humanity so that by his death he might

break the power of him who holds the power of death — that is, the devil — and free those who all their lives were held in slavery by their fear of death."[25]

Destructive forces rob abundance from your life.

Without the freedom mentioned above, we fall prey to destructive forces. Besides worry, fear, strife, and unforgiveness, I believe the primary destructive force at work in our world today is living in the wrong time zone, either in the past and/or in the future. Remaining in a wrong time zone is absolutely detrimental to having a fulfilling life and the attainment of your high calling as a bright light to the world. Not only does it distract you from the abundance available to you today, but it's also a key instrument that the devil himself uses to get you off track, attempting to defeat you in every area of your life.

Wisdom trains your emotions.

Understand that I'm not suggesting we ignore the past or the future. To do so would be unwise. On the contrary, what we should do with the past and the future is approach it with the wisdom of God. We ask God for wisdom, believing He will give it to us,[26] and we apply principles founded on truth to every situation and decision. If you are led by wisdom, you will not be led by your emotions. Moreover, living by wisdom will then *train* your emotions to support the alignment of your will with the wisdom you receive from God.

Here is your checklist for the future.

I have created my checklist of the items I want to focus on that concern the future. How should we properly align ourselves today so that we may set ourselves up for greatness tomorrow? Here are some action items to accomplish for this purpose:

- ✓ Create short-term goals: zero to twelve months from today.
- ✓ Create long-term goals: twelve months to five years from today.

- ✓ Schedule events and appointments that promote each of the *8 Areas*. This goes for short-, medium-, and long-term goals.
- ✓ Create and maintain a life to-do list, otherwise known as an Expect Great Things (EGT) list.
- ✓ Invest into the future with your time and resources today.
- ✓ Plan strategic systems for new businesses and the growth of existing businesses.
- ✓ Establish strategic plans that develop partnerships with new team members. (Note: team members include our family members, business partners or co-workers, and friends.)
- ✓ Build partnerships to set up multiple streams of income. This is to get money working for you so that you're not working for money.
- ✓ Implement strategic plans that cultivate growth and coaching for existing team members.
- ✓ Create a list of "The Top 50 People I Want to Meet."
- ✓ Produce vision boards for each of the *8 Areas* of your life.

Once again, living dependent on the past or the future is nonproductive and will allow your emotions to run over you. Your emotions will beat you like a bass drum if you're stuck in the limitations of the past or the fear of the future. Your emotions will take you on a roller coaster with ups and downs, highs and lows, valleys and mountaintops, producing instability in your practical reasoning skills. The greater the instability, the more easily your emotions push you up and down again and again.

Bring your emotions into focus today.

Yes, God made you with emotions. And He never makes mistakes. Emotions are designed by God to *support* us. Thus, training your emotions is a fundamental priority when it comes to living a fulfilling life and reaching your high calling. That's why your focus is on today and on bringing your emotions into the *right* focus today.

Keynotes:

- Dreading the future and worrying about what may come your way means that you're living in a wrong time zone.
- There is wisdom in living in the future with the right perspective.
- The top destructive forces are worry, strife, and unforgiveness.
- Destructive forces can rob the abundance from your life if you let them.
- Train your emotions to be calm and collected — not too emotional nor lacking emotion. This takes work every day.

Section Two

PRACTICE

CHAPTER NINE

Introduction to Practice

In previous chapters, we briefly touched on the word *practice*. It may be a familiar word to us, but let's expand our understanding of that word with new ways to use it.

One of God's favorite words is *practice.*

With all my heart, I believe that practice is one of God's favorite words because it removes the pressure from us. Let me explain, starting with the definition of practice:

prac·ticeprak-təs\[27]

1. to perform or do habitually or usually
2. to follow or observe habitually or customarily
3. repeated performance or systematic exercise for the purpose of acquiring skill or proficiency
4. the action or process of performing or doing something

In an article on forming habits, James Clear writes, "You should treat failure like a scientist, give yourself permission to make mistakes, and develop strategies for getting back on track quickly."[28] This expresses the idea of practicing. It keeps you on the offense in life because you're still in control and can choose what happens. It implies that making a mistake or a poor choice doesn't mean that you're a failure. You play until you win! Practicing is a mind-set that keeps you from getting down on yourself. Having the mind-set that you're practicing in life also removes self-condemnation. In other words, if something doesn't end up the way you (or anyone else) expected, then don't worry or beat yourself up about it. Instead, know that it's just a part of the journey.

Let's put this into perspective with the *8 Areas* of your life. After we've defined some goals for these *8 Areas,* we start implementing systems and strategies to accomplish these goals and get us where we want to be. What we're doing is *practicing* each of these *8 Areas*. We practice our health plan. We practice our business plan. We practice our rest plan. But if we miss a few steps or fail to adhere to a certain part of the plan, the good news is that we're not doomed to fail all the time, nor are we defined by that failure because we were only practicing getting better. It's like taking lessons for something: the purpose is to learn and grow from them through practicing.

What is this book designed to do?

Please take a concentrated moment to read the next few sentences slowly. Avoid the temptation to rush through them, and instead, meditate on them. Practice these, and then practice more, as if you were building up a muscle or forming a new habit:

- Walk in the wisdom of God.

- Be led by the Spirit of God.

- Develop your faith.

In the following chapters, you'll notice how these three points will overlap in some ways because they are all interconnected. Putting each of them into practice, you'll also notice that they produce a skillful and intelligent discernment in you, along with a confident understanding of your life. This is for you *today*, for all *8 Areas*, both in the natural and in the spiritual. Again, this may sound super-spiritual at first, but, rest assured, it's very practical.

Developing your capacity to function in both the natural and the spiritual arenas takes practice, practice, and more practice. You practice with every decision you make. And, bottom line, that's what we're doing today: *practicing* to better ourselves in all *8 Areas* of your life.

CHAPTER TEN

Practice Walking in the Wisdom of God

Now that we've introduced an expanded understanding of the word *practice*, let's discuss what that looks like and how it affects today — *the big day*. For starters, we can *practice the wisdom of God* in our words and in our emotions.

Practice training your words.

When something goes wrong, *practice* training your words. The odds of something going wrong in the course of life are, let's just say, fairly high. The problems you face may even seem insurmountable, e.g., the medical report you just got or other bad news of a loved one you just received. Trials happen to all of us. Here's where the important training part comes in: How will you manage these trials? Your reaction, beginning with your words, can make or break your big day. It's crucial to practice training your words *today*.

Wisdom works in real life.

One day, right after I had surgery, my son called me to ask how I was doing. I said, "I've never been better." One morning, I lost a *tremendous* amount of money in the stock market. That afternoon, a friend called and asked how I was doing. I said, "I've never been better." Another time, my doctor called with a report that there was a spot on my lungs. Someone asked me how I felt about the bad news. I said, "I've never been better." There was also the day when I got a call that my son had been shot in the head. That one was a tough one. It took some time, but I could eventually say, "I've never been better." (By the way, his life was miraculously saved by prayer, the Carrollton Police Department, and the awesome medical staff at Parkland Hospital in Dallas.)

All this can sound silly when presented with such bad news. So why would I say, "I've never been better"? The truth is, that simple statement is a profound game changer. When someone asks me how I am doing, I have an opportunity to train my words, my emotions, and my intellect, and to develop my faith. Once again, it's about *practicing*.

Another way to define practice is to "train" or "grow." I am literally training myself, and, for example, "practicing wisdom," with my speech. I am *growing* in wisdom. When I practice, I grow. As a matter of fact, when I train my words, I first grow in my prayer life. Words are seeds. With our words, we prophesy over our future. We use *the big day* to speak into our tomorrow by training our thinking and training our words. This is what it means to practice walking in the wisdom of God.

I'm also rehearsing my future over and over. I'm not being ridiculous or crazy, as some people would think, but just the opposite. I'm doing what the Bible describes as calling "those things which do not exist as though they did."[29] In other words, I'm prophesying. I'm giving faith a voice. I'm declaring the greatness of God. I'm proclaiming the joy of the Lord. I'm releasing abundance. Even in the midst of a storm, when things are upside down, when nothing seems to be working — it's in those exact moments that you should start speaking of the greatness of God. Training your words is wisdom in action.

Problems are opportunities in disguise.

Opportunity. This word is essential. I encourage you to add it to your everyday vocabulary. When I face a problem, no matter what it may be, I no longer view it as a problem but an *opportunity*. In doing so, I've changed my perspective and prophesied over my future. When I say, "It's never been better," I'm defining the problem as an opportunity to get better — even better than it was before the "problem" happened.

Even now, if I'm walking through "the valley of the shadow of death, I will fear no evil; For You are with me"[30] — everywhere, in all *8 Areas* of my life. This is nothing but an opportunity for God to turn all things for my good.[31] When I say, "I've never been better," five things take place physically and spiritually:

- I'm training my emotions to be calm and in tune with what God is saying about the situation.
- I'm speaking truth over my day (prophesying).
- I'm training my thinking.
- I am releasing words of faith.
- Most importantly, I'm bringing God into that situation and allowing Him to be involved.

Start using "The Big Guns" checklist.

In the list below, I have written some examples of what I speak when my world has turned upside down.

- This is going to be my greatest hour.
- Greater is He that is in me, than he that is in the problem.
- I am blessed coming in and I'm blessed going out.
- The Lord is my Helper, and I will not fear.
- I will set my thoughts on "whatever is true . . . whatever is pure . . . whatever is lovely."[32]
- "Beloved, I pray that you may prosper in all things and be in health, just as your soul prospers."[33]
- No weapon formed against me will prosper.[34]
- The Lord is my Shepherd, and I shall not want.[35]
- God has not given me a spirit of fear, but of love, power, and a sound mind.[36]
- My God shall supply all my needs according to His riches in glory by Christ Jesus.[37]
- I cast all my cares upon my Lord for He cares for me.[38]
- Be strong and of good courage! Fear not![39]
- Whoever is born of God overcomes the world and this is the victory that overcomes the world—my faith.[40]
- For I am persuaded that neither death, nor life, nor angels, nor principalities, nor powers, nor things present, nor things to come, nor height, nor depth, nor any other created thing shall be able to separate me from the love of God.[41]

Remain calm in the midst of a storm.

Being calm in a storm is paramount and sets you up to make quality decisions based on facts and wisdom as opposed to unstable emotions. It keeps you from losing control of yourself and allows you to tap into the Creator of the universe—God. If I'm upset, distraught, a bundle of nerves, or riddled with fear, you don't want me as the captain of the ship. (Go to YouTube and watch a video on Captain Sully when he hit the birds and how calm he was in the midst of a tragedy.) Likewise, you don't want your emergency surgeon racked with emotions when operating on you or a loved one. You want him or her to be calm and collected, possessing good judgment and reasoning skills in fragile moments like that.

Life is your training simulator.

Perhaps you never thought of it, but every experience can be used as a training simulator for your emotions. For example, when you declare, "I have never been better" while in the midst of a storm, you are training yourself to look at it with the right perspective. It causes you to make better decisions and not freak out. That's everyday life right there. It's critically important to gain understanding about how to manage your thought life so that your emotions don't rule over you.

Use every experience as a training simulator for practicing the wisdom of God, being led by the Spirit of God, and developing your faith.

Use the "4-to-1 Rule" when making decisions.

Anytime I begin analyzing the details of a decision, I always look for the negatives first, the reasons why it won't work. Once I discover all the negatives, then I see how many positives there are in making that decision. The rule: I need at least four positives for every negative if I am going to move forward with that decision. (I use this rule about 95 percent of the time.) For example, if I see four negatives to a particular decision, then that means I need at least sixteen positives. That rule or system is phenomenal. And it's so simple.

Beware of the ingredients of a bad decision.

Any combination of the following characteristics and situations can be detrimental to the making of a great decision. If you find yourself experiencing these, take some time to recalibrate your thinking and emotions before making a decision:

- Feeling an urgency to "make a decision right now"
- Being sloppy or disorganized
- Being loosey-goosey (careless, noncommittal)
- Being extremely emotionally charged
- Being emotionally disassociated
- Feeling freaked out
- Feeling nervous or overanxious (a bundle of nerves)
- Being fearful about the outcome
- Having to meet a deadline
- Receiving devastating news
- Hyperventilating
- Feeling "scared out of your mind"
- Being emotionally distraught
- Walking in strife with others
- Being upset
- Reading or listening to the news
- Starting to play the what-if game
- Questioning God
- Being upset with your spouse or friend
- Following the crowd
- Expecting the worst
- Overindulging in junk food
- Overindulging in alcohol
- Consuming illegal drugs or overly consuming prescription drugs that alter your thinking
- Feeling pressured by a friend or loved one
- Feeling intimidated
- Being lazy or lacking discipline

- Being extremely agitated
- Feeling exhausted
- Being money-motivated
- Having a mind-set that it's "greener on the other side"
- Feeling that it's a once-in-a-lifetime opportunity
- Living from the negative experiences of your past
- Living in fear of the future
- Rushing past the beginning

Learn the ingredients of a wise decision.

Now, how about some recipes for making great decisions? Possessing these qualities, disciplines, principles, etc. actually puts the odds in your favor:

- Consistently walking in *God's* wisdom
- Being led by the Spirit of God
- Having wise counsel — this is big!
- Using the "4-to-1 Rule"
- Lining your actions up with the Word of God
- Spending sufficient time in the beginning of an endeavor
- Being uncomfortable but not fearful
- Developing a plan for each type of decision
- Training yourself to be emotionally stable in the decision-making process
- Being able to laugh at yourself
- Being willing to stretch your current belief system so that you can rise to a new level
- Not overly focusing on the past or the future
- Sensing the peace of God
- Stretching your faith
- Having a Powerful Learning Agenda (PLA)
- Practicing discipline and self-control
- Having an articulated plan and written goals
- Being willing to do something you've never done, which is beneficial to you and/or others
- Not trying to be perfect
- Intending to practice getting better in that endeavor

- Visualizing the outcome
- Doing what most people would consider strange
- Being organized and neat
- Walking in the fruit of the Spirit of God

Wisdom and God's Spirit are practical.

Practicing the wisdom of God is, in fact, practical in everyday life. Wisdom brings order into every area of your life, especially when the Spirit of God teaches you how to recognize and use that wisdom. Learning to be led by the Spirit of God in the practice of wisdom is essential, which brings me to my next point: *practice being led by the Spirit of God.*

Keynotes:

- One of God's favorite words is *practice*.
- Practice removes condemnation.
- Practice is simply doing something again and again to grow in your ability to do whatever it is. That's what we do in life.
- Practice training the words that come out of your mouth.
- Practice not focusing on or rehearsing the problem.
- When someone asks how you are, practice responding with, "I've never been better."
- Your words have power over your day and your future.
- The words you rehearse affect your prayer life.
- Training your words, emotions, and feelings (regardless of the circumstances) gives you stability in the midst of the storm.
- Remove the word *problem* from your life and call it an opportunity. This is big.
- Practice being calm in the midst of the storm. Attach yourself to God's peace.
- Your words are seeds that create your future.
- Go over the recipe checklist for bad decisions.
- Go over the recipe checklist for wise decisions.

CHAPTER ELEVEN

Practice Being Led by the Spirit of God

When we practice something, it means that we are growing in it with the freedom to make mistakes and learn from them. On that note, *practice* building your relationship with God in each of the *8 Areas* of your life. How? Practice God's wisdom, being led by the Holy Spirit in each of those areas.

No matter what stage of the *8 Areas* you're in today — whether the beginning, the intermediate, or the mature — just start practicing your relationship with God in each decision *today*. As I mentioned, each area relates to both the spiritual and the natural dimensions of life. God is as involved in the natural as He is in the spiritual. His desire is to be in all places, in all decisions, and in everything that concerns you. The more you walk in God's wisdom, led by His Spirit, the more you build your relationship with Him. It takes practice.

One of the greatest challenges we face is ourselves.

If we're not led by God's wisdom and Spirit, then there are two primary ways we end up becoming our own worst enemy. It gets worse the more we enable these behaviors and thought patterns.

First, let me introduce you to Mr. Prima Donna, who is full of himself. One of his favorite phrases is, "Yeah, I know that!" Here are some of his characteristics and thought patterns. See if you recognize him.

- I know God had something to do with it, but I'm the main reason I had success.
- I'm the one who worked hard and studied. I put in the blood, sweat, and tears. Of course, a few other people had something to do with my success and greatness, but bottom line, I know it was really me.

- Look at me and look what I have accomplished! Look at how amazing I am because of my great self-discipline and what I have done.
- I am an entrepreneur; I am good looking; I am sharp, and I am a powerful person — that's why it's all about me, me, me!
- My family, my business associates, and my friends are so blessed that I'm in their lives.
- I have so much to say but so little time to say it.
- I'm just a wonderful person.
- Let's talk about me. Go ahead and tell me three reasons why I'm so wonderful. I know there are many more, but you can start with just three.
- Everything good that happens to me comes from what I created. Yeah, I may have had some help along the way, but it was really up to me.
- Of course, I'm humble! I know God is really blessed to have me on His team.
- I really have my act together. I don't cuss; I don't smoke; I don't do ugly things; I don't drink, well, just every now and then. I'm just a great individual.
- I go to church and Sunday school, and I'm very rich. Let's face it, I'm a blessing to everyone here!
- Well, I don't have to follow all the rules all the time. A little white lie is OK every now and then because of all the good I have done.
- What company wouldn't be grateful to have me? I set record after record of greatness.
- Obviously, I always fly first class. Only the commoners sit in the back.
- So what if I'm a little rude or a little short to that person? They were a waste of my time. Don't you know how valuable my time is?
- My time and I are just too valuable. I'm worth more per hour than you can afford.
- I noticed you can't keep from noticing this beautiful diamond ring I am wearing or this beautiful gold watch

on my left hand. Do you have any idea how much those items cost? Oh, by the way, that beautiful luxury automobile is mine. Want me to show you a picture of my luxury home?

- Don't you know my title? You don't have any idea who you're talking with right now and how important I am.
- Yes, I'm expecting to be recognized as superior. I deserve it.
- Yes, I'm a high-status individual.
- I have no doubt other individuals are envious of me.
- You don't have to tell me, I already know!

Wow, no thanks! I know it sounds exaggerated when written, but these types of attitudes and thoughts creep in more than we think and can prove to be one's own greatest challenges. It's time to align yourself with something greater: the wisdom of God! Mr. Prima Donna misses out on the greatness of *the big day* with a dangerous self-focus and self-promotion, meanwhile always ending up isolated from others. Wisdom, however, produces genuine humility and sets you up for success every day—in all *8 Areas* of life. That's a win-win!

It would be great if that's all we had to watch out for, but becoming our own greatest challenge doesn't end there. Meet Debbie Downer, who is always complaining about something. Here are some of her characteristics.

- We don't need to make too much money, just enough to get by.
- It's OK to be poor; it's normal.
- I can't do that—I'm not smart enough.
- I don't have what it takes. I know I'm going to fail.
- I've made way too many mistakes to move forward.
- I am too old now.
- I don't have enough money.
- There's not enough time in the day.
- I tried that before and it didn't work, so I'm not going to try again.

- You don't understand; that's not who I am.
- Maybe I'll do it someday.
- I am confused.
- That's too hard; I won't even try.
- It's too hot. It's too cold. I can't today — it's raining.
- It's never the right time to accomplish better things. I'll just wait.
- I'm too scared and afraid.
- What if I lose all my money?
- Oh, that doesn't work. I had a friend who tried that and look what happened to them!
- A little white lie is OK.
- It's definitely not my fault that . . . .
- I am so tired.
- I'm just simple countryfolk.
- I may be poor, but . . . .
- They make me so mad.
- Success is not what it's cracked up to be.
- No one should have to work that hard.
- I would rather spend more time at home.
- That makes me feel uncomfortable.
- It's my boss's fault.
- What's the use?
- You don't know what happened to me last year. It was horrible, devastating, and disastrous. I barely survived.
- I feel miserable. I'm so sad and too depressed.
- People don't appreciate what I've done for them.
- There's no guarantee I won't fail.
- You're right. I could never do that.

There's not a day that goes by that I have not been one of those two people I just mentioned. Reality is, we've all been both Mr. Prima Donna and Debbie Downer in one way or another. Sometimes, they even show up together disguised as Mr. and Mrs. False Humility.

So, what's the answer? The answer is to understand that you are great simply because of the grace (power and ability) of

God. Everything you have, everything you are, and everything you will be is because of the grace of God. Every breath you take is because of the grace of God. It will also take the grace of God to be the life coach to many that you were made to be. Take your eyes off yourself (whether Mr. Prima Donna or Debbie Downer) and recognize that your calling to be a coach is way bigger than you. Shifting this focus takes practice and work every single day, but it's worth it.

Yes, there is a fine line between Mr. Prima Donna and Debbie Downer. You might find yourself manifesting one and then manifesting the other a minute later. That is why we practice working on ourselves every day — morning, noon, and night.

The point is, if you want to *win big*, then practice being led by the wisdom and Spirit of God! I cannot emphasize this enough. Not only will it properly align you in life, but you'll also grow in relationship with Him as well as with others in the process.

In what other ways can we practice being led by God's Spirit?

Ask yourself the "5 Most Important Questions."

A number of years ago, a friend flew me to Kansas City in his personal jet to speak to a group of people about finances. I had a presentation prepared, which I've used for many years, to teach on how to build wealth. As I was sitting in the Marriott, I believe I heard the voice of God (not audibly, but more internally audibly, in my spirit). I heard Him tell me that He wanted me to teach on "the five most important questions you should ask yourself each day." Honestly, my first response was, "Absolutely not, God! I would need to prepare for that." He said, "No, it's really simple," to which I replied, "OK, I like simple. So, what are they?"

Listed below are the "5 Most Important Questions" which, I believe, you should form a habit of asking yourself.

1. What are you expecting today?
2. How do you see yourself today?

3. What are you doing today to improve yourself?
4. What words are you speaking today to frame your future?
5. Are you treating this as the most important day of your life?

In addition to these questions, I usually think of five things I am thankful for today. I then turn those five things and the five questions into a prayer, directing my thoughts to God and inviting His Spirit to speak to me concerning all these.

It's a great way to start your day. I normally do it when I'm shaving. I even have a conversation with myself. For example, I will say, "Mr. Whipple, what are you expecting today? I'm glad you asked." Then I will start answering that question. Again, it's a training mechanism for my spirit and my intellect, for my spiritual and my natural faculties. They are meant to work hand in hand. By the way, I don't do this seven days a week, but typically five. I like to change things up!

As an example, I've written down some ideas of how I see myself. In a sense, this is a list of various affirmations answering the questions, "Who are you?" and "Why not you?" I have developed this list over time as I have learned and practiced how to retrain my thinking. I believe the Holy Spirit spoke many of these to me, and I now speak these over myself several times throughout the week. I encourage you to make your own list and do the same. Train yourself to be inspired. Practice being led by His Spirit in the way you see yourself.

This is how I practice seeing myself, which affects all *8 Areas* of my life:

I see myself as a:

- Successful investor
- Philanthropist
- Great sower of finances and seeds
- Wise coach to my team
- Prayer warrior

I see myself as:

- Accountable
- Transparent
- Authentically humble
- Influential
- Very thankful and grateful
- Graceful in victory and opportunity
- Emotionally stable
- The head, not the tail
- The victor, not the victim
- Vision-oriented
- Creative

I see myself:

- Made in God's image[42]
- Walking in God's wisdom
- Being led by the Spirit
- Making quality decisions
- Developing my faith to do the impossible
- Empowering others to become leaders
- Taking the initiative in all *8 Areas*
- Thinking outside of the box ("If it's not broken, break it.")
- Embracing the discomfort of growth
- Consistently practicing a disciplined lifestyle in all *8 Areas*
- Training my words with greatness
- Expecting the best (the "law of attraction")
- Being a light to all (laying down my life[43])
- Refusing strife in my life
- Practicing forgiving others
- Using the "4-to-1 Rule" on all decisions
- Practicing walking in the fruit of the Spirit[44]
- Staying calm in the midst of a storm
- Leading people to a saving knowledge of Christ Jesus

- Living in the right time zone: living each day as the most important day of my life
- Not living on the mistakes or bad decisions of yesterday (getting over them and moving on)
- Putting on the full armor of God[45] each day
- Believing that no weapon formed against me will prosper[46]
- Attracting great team members who are accountable, have integrity, take the initiative, follow the systems, create better systems, and have a great work ethic in all *8 Areas*
- Confidently trusting the Lord with all my heart and not leaning on my own understanding

I see myself having:

- A warrior mind-set (physically, mentally, emotionally, and spiritually)
- Understanding and intelligent discernment
- A high net worth (money working for me instead of me working for money)
- Integrity that is second to none (no matter what)
- Multiple streams of income
- A great work ethic in all *8 Areas*
- A healthy lifestyle
- A ferocious PLA
- Outstanding alignments
- Incredible resolve (looking at a problem as an opportunity to better myself)
- Great peace (daily practicing the choice to live without fear or worry and being "anxious for nothing"[47])
- Great communication skills
- Non-judgmental attitude
- Great delegation skill sets
- Building a great team around me
- Effective plans, checklists, systems, and goals for all *8 Areas*

The spiritual force has natural advantages.

What is one of the decided advantages of retraining your thinking according to the wisdom and Spirit of God? In my opinion, it's definitely your physical stamina. The internal changes directly affect your propensity to thrive in two external ways: your exercise program and what you put in your mouth. Keep in mind that the reward of all this is an abundant life, as well as becoming a bright, bright light to everyone around you!

You're a walking testimony.

Your body is like a billboard advertising who you are and the way you think. If you haven't already, today is *the big day* to decide to get serious and proactive regarding the physical testimony of who you are. All too often, we know what to do, and we choose not to do it. That's going to change today.

Be aware of what you put in your mouth.

Make a conscious decision to educate yourself about what you eat and drink. Start doing research. Start reading labels. I know there's conflicting information out there, but be consistent about staying informed. On a regular basis, check the facts before you buy the product. Determine whether it fits your health plan and the direction of your goals. I'm not saying you can't have a piece of pizza or a hamburger every now and then; however, being assertive about understanding what goes in your mouth and how it specifically affects your body will keep you on the offense when it comes to your health.

Start with making a list of the ten healthiest foods for your body. Then post it on your refrigerator or something similar so you can see it every day.

Make exercise a top priority.

After you've positioned yourself on the offense with what you put in your mouth, the next step is developing your exercise program. It is critical — did I say critical? — to exercise a minimum of four times per week, including at least two core and two cardio workouts.

Obviously, before you start any special exercise program, get approval from a medical professional. Another important point: start slowly, slowly, slowly when beginning your exercise programs. Be knowledgeable about these programs too, as well as stretches and food and liquids that should or should not accompany the exercises.

In my opinion, you should go online and pull up the advantages of exercising and why it's so important. I highly encourage you to do this and see it for yourself. No doubt it will be a game changer — you'll get motivated, and you'll also enjoy what you learn. The medical industry lists dozens of advantages of exercise.

Practice being led by God's Spirit and wisdom when it comes to creating, preparing, and implementing a health plan that's best for you. To help you get started, I've listed fifteen healthy habits on the next page that will improve your overall quality of life.

15 HEALTHY HABITS

Use this checklist to train yourself to improve your physical quality of life. These are not in order of importance.

1. Get A-Z examinations: physical, dental, skin, etc. This puts you ahead of the curve and on the offense when it comes to your health. (Note: if you don't like your doctors, find ones you do like.)
2. Drink a lot of water every day. Do research on how much your body specifically needs.
3. Wash your hands thoroughly a minimum of four times per day.
4. Keep your hands (and pens or pencils) away from your face and mouth.
5. Take a deep breath a minimum of four times per day.
6. Exercise four times a week with at least two cardio and two core workouts. Include five minutes of stretching after each workout session.
7. The Bible talks about being "anxious for nothing."[48] Train yourself in this daily. Don't take on fear; instead, take on the peace of God. Train yourself to be calm and relaxed, even in the midst of a storm. Don't hang around the junkyards of worry, fear, or anxious thoughts.
8. Read your Bible daily. Use it to develop a great PLA to retrain your thinking and paradigms. This also detoxes all the junk we've unfortunately been trained to believe.
9. Eat fruits and vegetables every single day.
10. Get a minimum of six-and-a-half to seven-and-a-half hours of sleep every night. However, if you feel yourself getting sick, ramp up your sleep for one week.
11. Educate yourself on what you eat, being well-informed to make wise choices.
12. Get on a great vitamin or supplement program.
13. Train your words: speak life over yourself and others.
14. Take time to pray and meditate on God every day. Get quiet! Turn everything off for a minimum of five minutes twice daily.
15. Laugh every day — not just a small laugh, but big laughs.

Keynotes:

- Ask yourself the "5 Most Important Questions" when you're getting ready in the morning.
- With your words, rehearse the greatness you expect to see in your life when you're getting ready for the day (see examples on pages 86-88).
- Build your physical, emotional, and mental stamina.
- Be proactive about developing the physical testimony of who you are (your body).
- Study and know which kinds of food and liquid are harmful for your body to consume.
- Make a list of the ten healthiest foods for your body.
- Exercise a minimum of four times a week with at least two cardio and two core workouts.
- There are over fifty benefits of exercise. Research those.
- Two of the greatest challenges we face: becoming Mr. Prima Donna and/or Debbie Downer.
- Everything we have is by the grace of God.
- Practice going to work on yourself every day.

CHAPTER TWELVE

Practice Developing Your Faith

Faith affects the natural arena as much as it affects the spiritual. Faith is a belief that can transfer the spiritual into the natural, and it's a choice you need to make every day. Faith also refers to a spiritual substance; nevertheless, it takes a practical process of development to mature in the use of it.

Similar to building up a muscle, the process of achieving your goals can take days, weeks, months, and even years. However, as you train yourself mentally, physically, and spiritually, you position yourself to possess greater potential, like running a marathon. Faith works the same way. Faith takes a maturing process. Maturity doesn't happen overnight or instantly.

I recommend that you don't throw your faith away after experiencing disappointment like many others have; instead, use faith in the realm for which it was intended. Develop yourself with the wisdom of God ("practice" wisdom). Practice being led by the Holy Spirit, and then start working with your faith. Take it one step at a time. Then you will begin to see results.

Faith is one of the most misunderstood areas.

I believe the content covered in this book so far bears repeating for the purpose of building up your life. The subject of faith is one of those critical topics. There is no question that faith plays a substantial and fundamental role in your everyday life—big time.

The Bible describes faith as "the substance of things hoped for, the evidence of things not seen."[49] Wow, that is so good. Sadly, however, the mistake is made when we quote Bible verses, believing for something that is not seen, and then we rush past the beginning of an endeavor. We make the decision to move forward, but we fail to plan it out and get prepared for what's ahead.

I've especially noticed this with particular groups of Christians who have a certain understanding of faith. Using our faith without the wisdom of God in the planning ends up in a train wreck more often than not. Then we blame God and/or blame "faith" and say it doesn't work, and then we align ourselves with unbelief and disappointment.

Consequently, we end up limiting *the big day* as well as the future. In reality, we simply misunderstood what faith is: a spiritual substance given by God for us to steward. We fail to see that faith is not at its best when we rush past the planning stage and when we neglect to align our measure of faith with the wisdom of God and being led by His Spirit.

(Having said that, I know there are times when you will totally have to rely on faith, and no logic in the world will work with it. It won't be logical. But it *will* be the wisdom of God and the following of His Spirit to step out with it.)

Don't rush past the beginning.

If you have a hectic schedule, you often find yourself so fixated on getting back home at the end of the day or being a slave to your schedule throughout the day. Building your faith doesn't include a seeming urgency to get home or the strict adherence to a schedule. Many times, this leads to the fundamental mistake of always rushing past the beginning of other important endeavors.

Your schedule is essentially a system to keep you from wasting time on unproductive activities, and it's put in place for you to be more productive. It's not meant to be the leader of your life.

Anytime you have a choice to do something, be cautious of any sense of pressure to rush the decision-making process. Feeling rushed is a mind-set. You might not have a lot of time to make some decisions, but if that is the case, your decision should not be aligned with feeling rushed, especially if your daily life consists of rushing here, rushing there, listening to an inner voice that pressures you into thinking, *Quick! Quick! I've got to go now!*

Stop and slow the process down!

Well, you might say, "You don't understand. I have forty-five things to do today!" I'm telling you, "Slow down." I'm not saying to stop working. I'm talking about being methodical — don't be in a rush to be in a rush. Slow down and do the small things right — not tomorrow, and not just right now, but consistently. Plan and be prepared. Practice developing your faith to succeed and make the right choices. You will enjoy the fruit of it.

How do we end up in all the wrong places?

I have been in bad circumstances many times because of my own dumb decisions. Did I say dumb decisions? I'm sure we've all been there.

Oftentimes, we have the audacity to blame God, faith, other people, or the nature of the circumstances. Then we say ridiculous things like, "This must have been God's will," and, "He must be punishing me because I needed it." In reality, we ended up in that place by virtue of our own bad decisions.

Stop blaming God or faith, or even calling it an "act of God." Those are words we tend to use as insurance, keeping us from admitting the possibility that we made a mistake. When we misunderstand faith and how to combine it with the wisdom of God, we oftentimes end up in the wrong place. (But the fact that today is *the big day* means we don't have to stay in all the wrong places!)

God may or may not be closing the door.

I hear things like, "God must be closing the door," or, "God is opening the door." Don't let circumstances alone, whether good or bad, define the nature of what is happening or why. An open door doesn't necessarily mean God wants you to walk through it, and a closed door doesn't necessarily mean He doesn't have a strategy to get you through it.

I have been there too, thinking the supposed open door was a once-in-a-lifetime opportunity and therefore it must be God. Many of those times, I couldn't have been more wrong. If we're getting to the root of the issue, I was really led by my appetite to make a lot of money. It had nothing to do with practicing faith or being led by God. I think you know what I mean.

It can be hard to determine if an open door is the right one. This is where the importance of slowing down comes in so that you don't "rush past the beginning." So, how are we supposed to make a quality decision? I'm so glad you asked.

Classify your decision into one of three categories.

When I need to make a decision, I classify it into one of the following three categories:

- Decision A is a major decision.
- Decision B is an important decision.
- Decision C is an intermediate or small decision.

The processes for each of these decisions are important. On pages 98-100, you'll find the checklists I recommend. But first, let's discuss the importance of staying in a position to make quality decisions.

Be in a position to be in a position.

Avoid the emotional roller coaster. I've jumped on that more than once, and I normally end up finding myself in the wrong place at the wrong time. So, here's the premise: I want to keep myself in a position to be in a position to make wise decisions. It is so simple.

In other words, I want to already be ready to make a wise decision no matter when the opportunity arises. I want to stay positioned and aligned with wisdom at every moment. This will position me rightly so that I don't make impulse decisions.

Since life is an adventure, let's take a roller-coaster ride for example. (This has nothing to do with the emotional roller coaster I just mentioned.) Now that we've begun the adventure, we decide which ride we want to go on, and then we stand in the line for it. We know what's ahead of us because we know which ride we've chosen, which is like knowing a direction in life we're taking.

Once it's time, you strap in and get ready—you position yourself. You don't know the exact moment when the ride will start, but you know you'll be ready for it when it comes. You don't stand to the side, and, once the roller coaster starts moving, rush to jump into the seat and strap in for the ride. That would be dumb, let alone illegal!

That goes for life too. We shouldn't do that to ourselves. Instead, let's prepare ourselves by *staying* in alignment with wisdom at all times (strapping ourselves into wisdom), so that when the ride starts moving—when life starts moving, when seasons change, and when you need to make new decisions— you're ready. You're in a position to be in a position.

I know that what I'm about to cover is going to take some work, time, and discipline; however, it will save you from a lot of grief, human torture, torment, and hell on earth. I give you my word of honor: if you follow the systems on the next couple pages, then you'll make the right, quality decision a majority of the time. Start practicing this today.

DECISION-MAKING CHECKLIST

(Three types of decisions)

1. Major decision:

- Give it a minimum of ninety days before making that decision.
- Talk to three people from your wise counsel board. (See page 104.) Meet them face-to-face and take notes. Go over the pros and cons. (Note: This is not a counseling session. Don't turn it into counseling for the same reason many people do: they want to have other people tell them what to do so that when they do it and the counsel doesn't work out, then they have someone to blame.)
- Do diligent research, making great keynotes as you go.
- Use the "4-to-1 Rule."
- Confess over yourself that you have the wisdom of God and the leading of the Holy Spirit to see what you need to see and to have the understanding needed for that decision. Then receive it and believe it.
- Examine your choices to see if/how they align with biblical principles and the goals you set for each area of your life.
- Only after all that, I would recommend praying and fasting.
- Let your prayers align themselves with God's promises regarding that decision.
- Confess (believe and speak) that you know what to do based on God's wisdom and the leading of the Holy Spirit.
- Then take time to be still and quiet and listen to the "still small voice"[50] of God in your spirit.
- Most importantly, don't be rushed!
- If you have a "check" in your spirit, do not go forward with that decision. Be led by the peace of God.

2. Important decision:

- Give it a minimum of thirty days.
- Talk to two people from your wise counsel board either face-to-face or by phone for at least twenty to thirty minutes. Go over all the pros and cons. Take notes. (Remember, this is not a counseling session.)
- Do an intermediate amount of research, not too heavy but not too light. Again, make useful keynotes of the facts.
- Use the "4-to-1 Rule."
- Confess over yourself that you have the wisdom of God and the leading of the Holy Spirit to make a quality decision. Then receive it and believe it.
- Examine your choices to see if/how they align with biblical principles and the goals you set for each area of your life.
- Spend some time in prayer, being still and quiet before God, listening to His voice.
- Then pray about it. Don't just ask God about it but firmly believe that He will show you which direction to go.
- Don't be in a rush to make the decision.
- Make sure you have a peace from God before moving forward with your decision.

3. Small to intermediate decision:

- Give it a minimum of one week.
- Talk to one or two people via telephone for approximately fifteen minutes, going over the facts and details and the pros and the cons.
- Do medium to light research, making keynotes as you go.
- Use the "4-to-1 Rule."
- Believe and confess over yourself, "I have the wisdom of God, and I am directed by His Holy Spirit."

- Examine your choices to see if/how they align with biblical principles and the goals you set for each area of your life.
- Then be still and quiet before God, and pray about that particular decision, listening to His voice.
- Make sure you have a peace from God before moving forward with your decision.

I know what you're thinking.

"If I wait that long, I could lose out on that opportunity."

For example, you might be deciding on a house or accepting an offer for a job, etc. That's why it's critical to do your research beforehand, so you know what you're getting into and so that you're ready to make a quality decision when the opportunity arises. Remember: position yourself to be in a position.

When I sold real estate, I often showed properties to clients looking for a boathouse. Almost every time, they only considered the boat and the boathouse, but the reality was that there was also a house attached to that property with a boathouse. But they didn't pay much attention to that house, nor did they consider it a significant part of their decision. They were willing to spend hundreds of thousands of dollars for a boathouse. Talk about an emotional decision!

Develop your bulldog faith.

A bulldog with a bone knows two things: it's his bone, and he's not going to let it go. He's determined and tenacious. After following the procedures on the checklist above, it's time to develop your "bulldog faith" muscle. This developmental process is going to take some time, but that's OK. It's important to build a sustainable foundation for your faith to grow on.

On another very important note, if you're going to reach the next level of leadership, it *will* take this bulldog-like faith and tenacity. It's a determined faith based upon God's Word and personal promises, His wisdom and the leading of His Spirit, and what He has in store for you today. This is when the real breakthroughs materialize.

Having a bulldog faith means looking at the impossible and believing the impossible, without wavering. It's your promise from God, so you're not going to let it go. You then practice wisdom, *consistently* doing the small things right, every day. This is when life gets fun, and you can literally say to yourself that it's not a boring day!

You might get stretched (which is actually good for you), but like Indiana Jones, you seize each day as an exciting and great adventure. Bulldog faith will stretch you physically, mentally, and spiritually, but you'll love the reward of maturing in each of those areas. Being stretched the right way always makes the process worth it.

Having a team helps build your faith.

Practice developing your faith also by learning from and/or investing in others. Such people become "team members" in your life. Your team expands into many areas; therefore, team members can be long- or short-term.

My second-best friend (besides God) is a team member. That's my wife. She's obviously a lifetime team member. Your family is your team. Your business partners and associates are your team. Your friends are your team members, and the individuals on your wise counsel board (see page 104) are team members.

But it doesn't end there. When you walk into a store and someone helps you, they become a temporary team member. When you meet someone for the first time and you exchange names, they can become a team member, even if that "relationship" only lasts a matter of minutes. I have received more thank-you cards than you could imagine from relationships built just because I reached out and asked someone what their name was.

When I'm at a restaurant, I always ask the waiter or waitress for their name and then, yes, they too become a team member. Let's say you're the one at a restaurant, and the waiter introduces himself to you. Your purpose is not to be waited on but to minister to him. How do you do that?

You smile; you're polite; you make eye contact. (Obviously, be wise and discerning about how to interact appropriately based on whom you're talking to!) Your whole purpose is to create a positive experience with that person, even if the interaction only lasts a few minutes or a few hours. It may open an opportunity for you to invest in their life.

Their experience with you could be especially important if the other person doesn't treat you well. You know it's ultimately because they are hurting, so if you see them as a team member, you can approach them differently. It's not based on what's in it for you, but how you can be a light for them. Seeing others as team members could totally change their day or life — and even yours.

Also, this may sound crazy, but just because someone doesn't know my name doesn't mean they can't be my team member. Many of my mentors are people I have only studied about through books and electronic media. Although I may never meet them in person, they are still my team members.

Everyone has the same calling.

Beyond a shadow of a doubt, I believe that one of your highest callings in life is to be a coach — a life coach for your team in all *8 Areas*. Don't misunderstand: your job is not to nitpick but to coach; your job is not to preach at your team members but to be a coach; your job is not to condemn or accuse but to coach; your job is not to criticize someone's flaws but to coach; your job is not to micromanage your team but to coach your team; your job is not to tell your team what to do but to lead them by example as their coach. Big difference!

Walk the talk.

The best coach always demonstrates the characteristics of a great leader, setting the standards of excellence with integrity and consistently doing the small things right. They take the initiative and are accountable to their team. A coach has great empathy and is a tremendous listener. The best coach has a deep love for their team. I love how the Bible describes love, what it looks like, and how it operates:

Love endures with patience and serenity, love is kind and thoughtful, and is not jealous or envious; love does not brag and is not proud or arrogant. It is not rude; it is not self-seeking, it is not provoked [nor overly sensitive and easily angered]; it does not take into account a wrong endured. It does not rejoice at injustice, but rejoices with the truth [when right and truth prevail]. Love bears all things [regardless of what comes], believes all things [looking for the best in each one], hopes all things [remaining steadfast during difficult times], endures all things [without weakening].[51]

The greatest coaches live by faith.

In many cases, I was the coach, but I learned more from my team members than they learned from me. Have you thought about who could coach you in something? Have you thought about whom you could coach?

Today is your *big day* to start coaching others and being an encouragement to people in all walks of life. Smile when no one is smiling. Forgive all who may have been unpleasant, even if they don't deserve it. Give an encouraging word when you don't feel like it. Be happy when no one is happy. Give permission for people to have a bad hair day. Drop grudges.

Faith allows a person to see others, as well as circumstances, from a higher perspective. That's why a great coach is a problem-solver. (Again, we call those "opportunities.") Great coaches have vision. Great coaches have systems and processes, and they use effective checklists. Great coaches always improve. And when it's all said and done, they end up receiving more than they give.

Founding a wise counsel board is essential.

What is a wise counsel board? Your wise counsel board is a group of individuals with whom you want to meet and align yourself who demonstrate wisdom in their own lives and encourage you in developing your faith.

Notice I did not say they are perfect people. To date, I have approximately twenty-five people on my wise counsel board. This takes time to develop. I am very selective and discerning about whom I choose to be a part of my wise council board, but I want people from all walks of life.

At the same time, developing a wise council board means you'll probably be asked to be on a board for others as well. I am also very careful when I contact my wise council board so as not to overextend their good graces in spending time with me. I know they often have a lot going on.

Know who is on your "A-team."

Jerry Jones, the owner of the Dallas Cowboys football team, gave me some great insight one morning when he said to me, "Always take care of the details — and I mean small details — when you're in business."

Now, truth be told, he was actually speaking to a few thousand people on the radio that morning, but what he said spoke volumes to me. It's as if he called me out by name and spoke directly to me! It was powerful, and, you guessed it, he became one of my team members.

I love team members who are big thinkers — way above average. My team is meant to challenge me to think bigger, and therefore, win bigger. Some of my team members include Walt Disney, Henry Ford, Helen Keller, Martin Luther King Jr., Abraham Lincoln, Sam Walton, my wife, and many, many more.

And what's better than having an outstanding "A-team"? Being on God's team! The benefits of being on His team never cease to amaze me. Among those benefits are His numerous promises.

One of those promises to me (and to everyone) is, "For I know the thoughts that I think toward you, says the Lord, thoughts of peace and not of evil, to give you a future and a hope."[52] This alone can change a life, yet it doesn't even scratch the surface of what He promises to those on His team. Thousands of other promises found in the Bible include those of wealth, health, wisdom, peace, comfort, joy, forgiveness, honor, protection, and the list goes on and on! We win even when it doesn't look like we win.

Faith gives you the power to let go.

The fruit of faith is peace, and peace takes the pressure off your shoulders. How can you remain calm in the midst of a storm? It won't be the easiest thing to do at that moment, but remaining calm is in the power of letting go.

Faith is what empowers you to let go of fear. Like standing in the eye of a storm, you can remain totally calm and peaceful while the storm rages around you. Faith will be the very thing that positions you to receive the power of God, enabling you to let go of what holds you back, and, instead, hold on to the peace that moves you forward and builds your faith even more.

Developing your faith is like bench-pressing with your spirit. There's pressure to it at first because, by faith, you're pressing through to let go of something you thought you needed. But utilizing the power of your will to let those things go will, in turn, release their pressure off you. In place of this pressure, you're now free to receive God's perfect peace. (Much better!)

When you're in the valley or in a storm, let His peace calm you and release the pressure. On the next page, I have included a list of ten things to let go of starting *today*. Build your faith by letting go of these and receiving peace.

THE POWER OF LETTING GO

Here's a checklist of ten things to let go of today.
Let go of these, and hold on to perfect peace instead.

- ✓ Let go of toxic people in your life.
- ✓ Let go of your past mistakes.
- ✓ Let go of the need to be right.
- ✓ Let go of feeling sorry for yourself.
- ✓ Let go of negative self-talk.
- ✓ Let go of the need to impress others.
- ✓ Let go of average beliefs.
- ✓ Let go of trying to please everyone.
- ✓ Let go of complaining.
- ✓ Let go of worrying about the future.

"Peace I leave with you; My [perfect] peace I give to you; not as the world gives do I give to you. Do not let your heart be troubled, nor let it be afraid. [Let My perfect peace calm you in every circumstance and give you courage and strength for every challenge.]"[53]

Keynotes:

- Faith plays a substantial role in your everyday life.
- Practice developing the proper faith muscles each day.
- Develop your "bulldog" faith.
- The beginning is important. Don't rush past the beginning, but, instead, *always* take the necessary time to firmly establish the beginning of any endeavor.
- Don't ever feel rushed when making a decision. Don't allow people or circumstances to rush you.
- Dumb choices equal turmoil and strife.
- Don't base your decision entirely on the circumstance itself.
- Put yourself in a position to be in a position.
- There are three main types of decisions: a major decision, an intermediate decision, and a small decision. All are important.
- Use the "4-to-1 Rule" for every type of decision.
- After asking God what to do, believe and speak over yourself that you have wisdom from God to know which decision to make.
- Develop your wise counsel board. This is something that you'll continue working on.
- We all have a calling to be a life coach (an encourager) to everyone.
- The best coaches have a deep love for their team.
- Your team members can be mentor figures you've never met. They should be big thinkers.
- Practice calling the things "which do not exist as though they did."[54] This is faith.
- Practice the ten points on "The Power of Letting Go" checklist.

Section Three

THE 11
CORNERSTONES

CHAPTER THIRTEEN

Introduction to the 11 Cornerstones

Applying to both the natural and spiritual forces, the topics and systems we've covered so far can dramatically improve your quality of life. When practiced consistently, they will help to prosper you in your finances, relationships, health, and even in your career. You will see stability taking root in all *8 Areas* of your life.

Now let's add to our foundation with the *11 Cornerstones* for reaching your high calling. These cornerstones play a major role in the unfolding of your life in both the professional realm and the personal realm. You will experience success from the intentional, premeditated use of these *11 Cornerstones*. It's about developing yourself from the inside out, allowing you to see improvement internally, externally, and eternally.

I'm reminded of a great scene in the story *Alice's Adventures in Wonderland*. In the sixth chapter of the book, Alice is walking down the road when she arrives at an intersection. Sitting at that intersection is the Cheshire Cat. I will paraphrase the conversation:

Alice asks, "Which way should I go?"

"It depends on where you want to get to," responds the cat.

Alice says, "I don't really care."

The cat replies, "Then it doesn't matter which way you go."

As a matter of fact, if we already set goals for the *8 Areas* of our lives, then we *do* know where we are going. Therefore, it *does* matter which path we take—not every path catapults us into greatness. Implementing these *11 Cornerstones* positions us in the direction that leads us to growth and more importantly, our high calling.

We could spend weeks writing volumes of books about each of the *11 Cornerstones*. Our priority here is to simply identify and outline them. As we progress, we will discuss them in greater detail, and relate them to your career, relationships, and other areas of life.

Contrary to the *8 Areas* of your life, the *11 Cornerstones* discussed below *are* in order of importance. Imagine the first five cornerstones as the vehicle you choose to move you forward in life. Cornerstones 6–11 relate to the fuel that fills up your vehicle. Here are your *11 Cornerstones*:

- Cornerstone 1 — Your Alignments
- Cornerstone 2 — Your Plan
- Cornerstone 3 — Your Thinking
- Cornerstone 4 — Your Disciplines
- Cornerstone 5 — Your Attitude
- Cornerstone 6 — Your Systems
- Cornerstone 7 — Your Resolve
- Cornerstone 8 — Your Accountability
- Cornerstone 9 — The 8 Areas of Your Life
- Cornerstone 10 — Your Work Ethic
- Cornerstone 11 — Thankfulness

Your journey is directly affected by the vehicle you choose.

My wife and I have lived in the Dallas-Fort Worth area for over thirty-five years. We currently live in Fort Worth, Texas. (By the way, we are big TCU Horned Frog fans. Go Frogs!)

So, this is the premise: let's say my wife and I are going to take a trip to California. Not too long ago, people would travel from Texas to California in covered wagons and it was perfectly acceptable, although many people did not make it.

Many others walked or traveled by horse, but the journey was just as treacherous. Nowadays, the options and forms of travel seem endless, with hundreds of different modes of transportation for people to choose from each day. We can go by bicycle, motorcycle, bus, train, plane, or automobile — not to mention the plethora of makes and models within each of those modes of transportation. Yet with all these modes available for our journey today, the vehicle we use may still cause us to question whether it can make it to the destination. Haven't we all been there?

That's the way life is.

Let's say we are all going to take a trip to a destination. In fact, let's say that this trip is a type and shadow of our life journey or, in other words, where we're going in life. We can choose the vehicle we want to travel in, but there's always the possibility that we'll end up somewhere else. (Should have asked for directions!)

Also, the quality and length of the journey will be dependent on the condition of the vehicle we choose to use. I would say that life is a journey constantly in motion, always going somewhere, whether we like where it's going or not. I think we can all agree with that.

The great news is, we as human beings can choose which vehicle we want to travel in every single day of our lives, except for situations beyond our control. Now I know we often think that we didn't choose our own vehicle, but in reality, many times we actually *did* have a choice.

Cornerstones 1–5 make up the vehicle you travel in through life.

Just as a vehicle is meant to move you forward, Cornerstones 1–5 describe the way your life is logically progressing, in the natural and in the spiritual. What I mean is that evaluating these five areas will tell you exactly how your life is going today: great, good, fair, poor, or in the abyss. What type of vehicle are you using? What is the condition of that vehicle, and in which direction is it headed? In other words, how is it progressing?

Let's think about this a minute. What is the natural progression of not taking care of the car you drive every day? It will die on you. Not immediately, but it's the natural progression of a thing. If I use my cell phone all day and don't charge it, the natural progression is that it will run out of juice. On the other hand, if I work out regularly and eat right every day, the natural progression is that my body becomes healthier. The first five cornerstones are a natural part of life, and each one has its own natural progression.

You will naturally progress into what your alignments, plan, thinking, disciplines, and attitude are. Whether you believe in the first five cornerstones is immaterial; they are still consistently operating in everyone's life every single day. That's why it's *critically important* to go to work on these cornerstones every single day, starting today. I suggest that you memorize them and engrave them on your heart so that it's your natural default to travel in the right vehicle and move in the right direction.

No doubt, they will prepare you for when you do face the storms of life, and they will certainly help you get through the storms. I would even go so far as to say that these five cornerstones can also alter the course of your journey and keep you from encountering certain storms of life. It's like taking preventative measures, as many of our storms are brought about by poor choices we made and poor disciplines to which we have been accustomed. Who wants to suffer unnecessarily? Yet, that's often what happens.

Cornerstones 6-11 are the fuel for your vehicle.

We can easily take for granted how important a role that fuel plays in our everyday life. Have you ever thought about that? Everything that moves needs some kind of fuel or energy to keep it moving. The same goes for your life's vehicle. How are you going to keep moving forward?

The answer lies in Cornerstones 6–11. But be aware of the quality of fuel you use. Using bad fuel can contaminate your engine parts, causing your engine to sputter or even stop your car from running altogether. (I once was on a motorcycle trip, and I unknowingly put bad fuel into my motorcycle. I have one word to describe that: nightmare!) After the vehicle, the type of fuel you use is everything.

The *11 Cornerstones* are foundational, strategic tools to help you reach your highest potential in life.

Making the most of *the big day* is all about reaching your highest potential in life. It's about going from upside down or average to above and beyond! The problem is, many of us *settle* for average or below average. All of the following are signs of an upside-down lifestyle which many people have experienced and/or are currently experiencing today.

- Being broke, financially not making ends meet, or being heavily in debt
- Constantly being sick
- Being in strife with your spouse or going through a divorce
- Being a slave to worry, fear, anxiety, food, pornography, alcohol, prescription drugs, and/or illegal drugs
- Being depressed or always angry; losing your job
- Not knowing what to do about a job, or not liking your job
- Feeling scared or afraid
- Being pregnant out of wedlock
- Always being in pain

The *11 Cornerstones* are not necessarily the answers, but they are certainly strategic tools that can help you when your life is upside down. In many cases, there are no easy answers or simple solutions, but start where you are today.

God can help you, and He always has a strategy that's perfect for you. I am convinced of that. He has always come through for me and will do it for you. So, take the first step. Then the next step. Take one step at a time. One day at a time. I will be praying for you and the other people reading this book. God is going to do great things through you. Your best is yet to come!

CHAPTER FOURTEEN

Cornerstone 1 – Your Alignments

Here's a million-dollar question: What is the number one key for you to live a fulfilling life? It's your alignments! Your number one priority is to have great alignments.

What you align yourself with is what you will become.

If you align yourself with great people, great books (i.e., the Bible), great movies, great television shows, great music, great investments, great expectations, great values, great mind-sets, great peace, and, of course, great football teams like the Horned Frogs (just kidding), you just raised the odds of significantly improving your thinking and, therefore, your quality of life.

On the other side of that coin, if you align yourself with junk, then that's exactly what you're going to become. Maybe not overnight, but trust me, you will begin (and gradually increase in) manifesting the qualities and character of everything and everyone with which you have aligned yourself. We naturally associate ourselves with our alignments.

Getting out of your current way of thinking helps you see your world in a different light. I love to spend time with the CEO of the entire world, God. "It is God who arms me with strength, And makes my way perfect."[55] What else does He do? "He trains my hands for battle, So that my arms can bend a bow of bronze."[56] He teaches me to win battles that would have been too much for me, and if that weren't enough, He gives me the strength to do it as well! The Bible also says, "The things which are impossible with men are possible with God."[57] Wow, talk about a big thinker! He's absolutely my number one alignment.

Be selective with your alignments.

Each year, advertisers spend billions of dollars to train you in what to wear, what gadget to buy, what to drink, how to live, how to act, etc. You get the picture. The answer is simple: don't hang around garbage. Negative people and influences are not going to help you achieve your dreams. This is your *big day*. Go for the gold in your associations. Be careful not to just follow the crowd, but instead, keep a high standard of excellence when it comes to choosing your alignments.

Your top three alignments are like your best friends.

These are my three best friends, or in other words, my top three alignments.

My number one alignment is God. Many years ago, I made a quality decision not to be a self-made man but a God-made man. Even though I'm headstrong and can be stubborn about having my own way, there is absolutely no way I will do life without God. For example, I might start certain tasks without even thinking about God, just because I'm good at what I do. But oftentimes I'll stop and go back to the beginning of that thing to make sure I get the wisdom of God instead of doing it my own way. I love spending time with the CEO of the world because He is such a *big thinker*!

My number two alignment is my second-best friend in the whole wide world. That's my wife. (I call her "Hot Lips." She's a nurse. If you know the show *Mash*, you know why I call her that.) I'll share with you what I tell everyone else: there are only two perfect people in the world—God and Nancy.

My third best friend—brace yourself—is StubHub. Thanks to StubHub, I've seen some of the best sporting events, games, and concerts in the country.

On another note, my wife's top three alignments are God, me, and . . . Neiman Marcus. (She wins the MVP award when it comes to shopping!)

Excuses rob the potential out of your big day.

What keeps you from making today your *big day* and reaching your high calling in life? Excuses. On the next page, I've given you the "Top 15 Excuses" with which you should never align yourself. (Remember how your words frame your future?) Remove these words from your vocabulary and never ever align yourself with them again, even when you're really tempted to believe them and speak them.

THE TOP 15 EXCUSES

Excuses are beliefs with which you should never align yourself. Starting today, remove these words from your vocabulary! Your high calling awaits you on the other side of these excuses:

1. Someday, I might try . . . .
2. That's not me.
3. You don't understand.
4. It's not my fault.
5. I've tried that.
6. I don't have the money.
7. It's hard.
8. I don't have the time.
9. I'm tired.
10. I've never done that before.
11. What if . . . ?
12. What is the use?
13. I'm too old.
14. I don't understand.
15. That's so unfair.

Cornerstone 1 includes the "Top 10 Spiritual Alignments."

The most important cornerstone in our lives is our alignments. I would like to share the "Top 10 Spiritual Alignments" with you. I would even say that these are part of God's will for each of our lives. I know that's a bold statement, but I believe it's true.

You could take weeks, months, and years to meditate on and study these ten spiritual alignments. I would encourage you to use your Bible and cross-reference each of the ten alignments with Scriptures. Find passages that support these alignments and inspire you to make them a part of your everyday life.

It's important to note that, although these ten spiritual alignments are spiritual in nature, they absolutely relate to and work with the natural. In fact, they *should* work with the natural. They should work with the natural every day, including Monday through Saturday — not just on Sunday. That's the way God originally intended it to be.

Spiritual Alignment Number 1: God's Grace.

We must do our best to fully comprehend and understand that every good thing we have in the past, in the future, and today is by the power of the grace of God. It starts with God's grace, not us. That's what makes *the big day* so powerful. It doesn't start with anything we have done, good or bad.

Religion teaches about "works," but works have nothing to do with grace. Religion teaches that it's about what you do or don't do, which engrains within us a performance mentality. But I'm saying that your walk with God is not driven by performance — it's built on God's grace because He loves you. That's the pecking order you have to get down. We do great works because of His grace at work within us. His grace and power are the source of the greatness we accomplish in our lives. In other words, it's not about how good you are but about His power and ability at work in you. God loves you just as you are *today*, and because of His love, His grace is there for you *today*.

Spiritual Alignment Number 2: Jesus did it all.

On Calvary, Jesus became the ultimate sacrifice, paying the ultimate price to bridge the gap between God and man. Nothing we have done and nothing we could ever do compares to this marvelous and wonderful truth.

Spiritual Alignment Number 3: You have the power to choose.

Once you consider the grace of God and the sacrifice of Jesus, the third greatest gift that God gave to humanity is free will, or the power to choose. We have been given the freedom to make choices. We therefore have a choice to commit our life to God, the choice to receive His life through salvation, and the choice to be self-controlled and disciplined. It's a powerful privilege, and one that we need to take seriously.

Spiritual Alignment Number 4: Develop your PLA.

This is your Powerful Learning Agenda. So far, we've talked a lot about retraining your thoughts and emotions. Your PLA will help you do just that. It's a plan you intentionally put together consisting of tools and resources that will help you continually progress in renewing your mind and emotions according to the wisdom of God.

Developing your PLA is crucial to your success. Like checklists, they keep you focused on, and accountable to, your goals. For example, read a certain number of books by the end of the year that would help you emotionally, spiritually, or relationally. Or, spend a certain amount of time each day or each week practicing skills that renew your mind.

Think of your thoughts and emotions as a building you are renovating. A PLA is like scaffolding. First, you know what areas are being worked on by where you set up the scaffolding. Scaffolding also provides structure for the renovation, and it's how you're able to work on hard-to-reach places. Your PLA is a steady support system for powerful thinking in all *8 Areas* of your life.

You'll have to choose what you include in this dedicated plan, but the important part is that you get your resources and plan together. Start developing your success agenda. We will discuss this more in *Chapter 16: Cornerstone 3 – Your Thinking.*

Spiritual Alignment Number 5: Grow in God every day.

Discussed in detail in the previous section, growing in God every day consists of developing and practicing three important areas:

    1) walking in the wisdom of God,

    2) being led by the Holy Spirit, and

    3) developing bulldog faith.

Spiritual Alignment Number 6: Develop and practice your prayer life.

Develop a prayer life with God. By that, I mean develop your communication with God. When we think of prayer, we often think of kneeling down, closing our eyes, and petitioning God with our words. That is a great way to show your respect to God; however, prayer means so much more than that.

Prayer is a form of a partnership with God. Prayer is two-way communication. Different types of prayer include repentance, surrender, prophecy, praise, worship, praying in tongues, intercession on another's behalf, as well as simply remaining still and quiet, listening to God. These are just a few forms of prayer, and yes, there are many more.

Spiritual Alignment Number 7: Stay focused on your assignments for each of the *8 Areas* of your life.

Here again are the *8 Areas* of your life. Remember that these points are not listed in order of priority. They're all equally important.

- Your health plan
- Your spiritual plan

- Your wealth plan
- Your family/friends plan
- Your career/school plan
- Your rest plan
- Your hobbies plan
- Your PLA plan

As mentioned, I have heard it said, "Put God in first place, your family in second place, and your career in third place." However, I'm saying that God doesn't just want to be in first place. God is everywhere all the time, and He wants to be involved in all 8 Areas of our lives, and in every stage of every area—beginning, middle, and end.

Staying focused on your assignments in each area begins with establishing some priorities. List out your three highest priorities for each of the *8 Areas* of your life. Then focus on those and get to work on them. Don't get distracted with the clutter that pulls you from your priorities.

Spiritual Alignment Number 8: See yourself as a champion, a warrior, and a victor.

The way you see yourself and God in you affects every area of your life. The voice you believe will determine your future. If you believe the voice of fluctuating feelings or past mistakes, you'll have difficulty seeing yourself as a champion and winning big in life. Fully grasping and comprehending that you are a victorious warrior takes practice and discipline.

Spiritual Alignment Number 9: Train your words.

"Death and life are in the power of the tongue, And those who love it and indulge it will eat its fruit and bear the consequences of their words."[58] Your words carry power. They are seeds that shape your future. Be aware of every word that comes out of your mouth. Don't automatically speak everything you think. Train yourself to speak life over yourself (including every area of your life), over others, and over situations.

Spiritual Alignment Number 10: Be a light for all to see.

Jesus spoke of "laying down"[59] your life. He was the greatest example of this and, therefore, the brightest light the world ever witnessed. Following this example of laying down your life also causes you to shine as a light for all to see. Laying down your life includes your resources—including your money and your time.

You inherently possess the high calling of being a bright light in the world, an instrument God can use every single day of the week, Sunday through Saturday, not *just* on Sunday. If you asked me to give you a brief definition of success, I would simply say: laying your life down for a greater cause. In this way, you reach your high calling as a light for all to see.

Keynotes:

- What you align yourself with is what you'll become.
- Be selective with your alignments.
- My number one alignment is God.
- Remove the Top 15 Excuses from your vocabulary. Do not align yourself with them any longer.
- Review and focus on the Top 10 Spiritual Alignments.

CHAPTER FIFTEEN

Cornerstone 2 — Your Plan

It becomes obvious to your team and customers when you are not operating with a plan. You chase your day like a balloon floating wherever the wind blows. A certain proverb says, "The plans of the diligent lead surely to abundance and advantage, But everyone who acts in haste comes surely to poverty."[60] Your plan consists of three areas: your appointments, your to-do lists, and your goals. We will now address these critical components in much detail through "The Big Day Time Management System."

Don't let time hold you hostage.

If you're an adult from any walk of life, no doubt you have experienced frustration in the area of basic time management, trying to balance priorities but seemingly never having enough time to accomplish the goals of the day. We rehearse within ourselves the idea that there's "just not enough hours in the day." Have you ever said that? Of course you have!

Most all human beings experience this same frustration. We're always feeling rushed and overworked, chasing our tails by the end of each day, which often carries over into the next day. Thinking we possess the solution, we start multitasking. In reality, we're probably "shallow-working," i.e., just touching the surface. All too often, it's not real productivity.

Then, here we are, starting a perfectly good day with every intention of making it productive and then—BAM—the door opens, the phone rings, and the next thing you know, all kinds of problems, distractions, "emergencies," and other unexpected priorities flood in and kidnap our day. It's like being held hostage. It's frustrating and demoralizing. And again, the clock ticks away and we find that another day has gone by, lacking the necessary hours to accomplish everything on the agenda. It's like we're living in the movie *Groundhog Day*, repeating the same day over and over.

What's the solution?

The problem is not that there's not enough time on any given day; it's simply the lack of an effective time management system with disciplined implementation, which serves as the number one culprit of not getting everything done or reaching your maximum effectiveness. So, let's back up a little bit.

How important is *the plan* for all *8 Areas* of your life and the disciplined implementation of that plan? I would say it's the number two priority and critically important for a successful life. This comes right after the priority of your alignments. Would you agree? Only after you've discovered and established the right alignments in your life can a plan and system work for you. But without the plan, the alignments get lost in ineffective time management.

Plan to have the time of your life.

Let me introduce you to "The Big Day Time Management System." This is nothing more than a system that permits ordinary people to achieve extraordinary results and grow in every area of life at the same time. Here we go:

SEE IT – PLAN IT – DO IT – EXPECT IT – REPLAN IT

"The Big Day Time Management System" is a simple, practical, and methodical way to help you take your life and the time available to you and turn it into the time of your life! You'll be able to move into capacities you never dreamed possible.

Beware of the time management disclaimer.

As you follow the principles of "The Big Day Time Management System" with due diligence, along with the wisdom and Spirit of God, be prepared for a life of adventure, fulfillment, purpose, inspiration, excellence, and opulence.

Most importantly, be prepared to see your high calling unfold before your very eyes.

For this system to work properly, you must apply yourself with discipline, consistently following the systems and program for the next ninety days. (Some research suggests that it takes ninety days to form a habit.) My commitment to you is that you will see a noticeable difference and improvement in all *8 Areas* of your life.

You were meant to flourish in all *8 Areas*—simultaneously.

Your life is made up of eight separate areas, all of which are important to a great life. Without a written, organized plan in all *8 Areas*, it is very unlikely that you will have true success. The majority of people worldwide do not have predictable success in all *8 Areas* of their lives. They may have success in one, two, or even three areas but not in all eight. I believe your God-given destiny is to experience greatness and fulfillment in *all 8 Areas simultaneously*, with each one operating effectively.

What's the catch?

If I had the opportunity to put up a roadblock across a major freeway, pull everyone over to the side, hold a camera and microphone up to each person's face, I'd ask them, "Do you want to be successful? Do you want a life full of greatness? Would you like to have a successful life that starts today?" I believe most everyone would answer with an emphatic, "Yes, absolutely! But what's the catch?"

How do we get this successful life? The catch is understanding that *simply wanting something is not good enough.* You must define, plan, focus on, and schedule specific actions and then do them with due diligence. The amazing power of choice can alter your life, especially when it comes to planning and accomplishing goals. By simply understanding the forces at work in the human body and mind, you will position yourself to have excellent time management skills and the greatest opportunity for success.

Balancing your life is not realistic.

In the real world, it is impossible to have true balance in all *8 Areas* of your life at the same time. For instance, there may be a time when you're going to school or starting a business, and you may need to dedicate more time to that area than the others. Let's say you're starting a business. You may have to work between seventy and eighty hours a week for the first two to three years. And what if you're in medical school? Obviously, you'll invest more in school than other areas.

The key is not to ignore the other areas of your life. You still plan for them. The fact is, you'll just have to be more strategic in your planning. Take my life right now for example. Even as I write this book, I'm also launching a new business, along with maintaining my other businesses, but the new business requires more concentrated time. Thus, I am very selective about how I spend my time.

Realistically, you should always be selective when it comes to what you do with your time. The wisdom of God and the Holy Spirit can literally and practically help you in being rightly selective with your time. Remember what we discussed about not rushing past the beginning? That goes for the planning process as well. Be strategic and don't be in a rush. (Did I say don't be in a rush?)

Instead of following your feelings, follow the plan.

Observing the lives of people in America, I began to recognize that the ability of a person to take control over their thoughts, words, and actions makes all the difference between success and failure, happiness and depression, as well as health and sickness. If you take this time management system and try it for only a few days, I give you my word of honor that it will not work. Instead, I encourage you to adopt an immigrant's posture: you must be hungry for change, *want* to change, and be willing to pay the uncomfortable, inconvenient price for the change.

We live in a society where instant gratification, comfort, and overindulgence reign supreme. It is not easy to gain control of our lives today when our senses are so bombarded with the world's attempt to seduce us into living according to what we feel. Following your feelings and emotions without the wisdom of God will result in nothing more than an emotional roller coaster.

Let's examine some of the fruit of a person with no systematic, written plan:

- Successful in one or two areas, but the rest are suffering
- Usually frustrated
- Often tired and complaining
- Inconsistent
- Lazy and lethargic
- Confined in financial jail, living week-to-week or month-to-month
- Riding an emotional roller coaster
- Messy home or car
- Average or poor relationships
- Destiny or purpose has not been defined
- Usually very negative
- Easily offended
- Disorganized
- Like a balloon, floating wherever the wind blows
- Stress and anxiety are their best friends
- Always feeling sorry for themselves
- Grumpy, irritable, and no fun to be around
- Possessing selfish tendencies most of the time
- Thinking and mind-set is influenced by the news

Find your time management tools.

Time management tools, especially electronic ones, are very effective in managing all *8 Areas* of your life. One of my preferences, called Easy Calendar, is an app on my smartphone. It is a simple and effective way to keep track of appointments, and it also integrates with the iPhone calendar. It's specifically designed for setting frequent appointments. With just two or three taps, you can create appointments, including its time and description. The other tool I use for my to-do list is the Notes app on my smartphone. It works extremely well for me.

With that said, you may want to experiment with several tools that suit your needs and preferences. Block out some time to learn about different tools and find what works for you. This will obviously take a little practice. Set up your workflow utilizing those tools and see how it goes. If you need to change it up, then that's OK, but at least you'll then have an idea of what kind of system you need as you move forward.

Effective time management begins with mapping out your time.

Setting up a strategic plan for managing your time involves four areas of *mapping* out your time and four areas of *planning* your goals. Let's go over the mapping first. Note that the mapping is necessary for all *8 Areas*.

1. **Dedicated appointments:** These are the appointments that you schedule in advance for all *8 Areas* of your life. Dedicate a time for these, including a specific start and end time, e.g., from 1–2 p.m. Below are just a few examples of what I set as dedicated appointments:

   - Work out (typically four times a week)
   - L-O: this stands for lights on, lights off. (Many overachievers don't recognize that the proper amount of sleep improves overall performance.)
   - Sit down for breakfast, lunch, and/or dinner with my wife (typically five meals a week)
   - Read
   - Football games
   - Ride my motorcycle
   - Goal planning
   - Business appointments

- PLA
- Prayer time
- Strategic wealth planning (Most people don't set appointments for themselves to build wealth. What do they end up doing? Working for money.)

2. **EGT list:** The second area of mapping is the to-do list, which I keep in my Notes app. I call it an EGT list, which stands for "Expect Great Things." The individual items on this list do not have their own dedicated appointment; however, I set dedicated appointments to accomplish tasks on the list.

    I rank them in order of priority using the letters A, B, and C. Obviously, A is the highest priority. I never try to remember anything, as I typically have at least two hundred items or more on my EGT list. My goal is to complete five items each day. They range from books I want to read, to people I want to call or meet, to specific action items for my businesses and personal life.

    When I am in the field with one of my businesses, I carry a clipboard with me in case I need to make notes to add to my EGT. (Sometimes, it's easier to write it down first and then add it to my phone later, especially when I'm talking with someone.)

3. **Goals:** There are hundreds of books written on goal planning. All of them carry a measure of truth and can be somewhat good for you. I believe the system put together in this book can be a gigantic game changer in your life when you discipline yourself to follow it for ninety consecutive days. We will explain this in more detail as we discuss your goals program (goal planning) and how much dedicated time you should spend on it.

4. **Designated checklist:** This refers to following the checklists which I have already created and designated for particular appointments. For instance, when I

exercise by myself, I have an exercise checklist that I follow. When I go out of town, I have a travel checklist, which includes what I pack. I also have a checklist of people I pray for each day of the month. Creating checklists for routine or frequent endeavors keeps you focused on the task set before you.

After mapping out your time, plan your goals.

To continue our time management system, I'll now share the four simple, practical rules for setting up and managing your time and goals, otherwise known as **planning**.

There are four times that I set aside to plan, review, and/or rearrange my goals and appointments. Typically, I spend the first three or so minutes of these times praying, specifically thanking God that I'm not led by the schedule, and that I have His wisdom and the leading of His Spirit to do what He wants me to do and when He wants me to do it so that I'm in the right place at the right time. Being in the right place at the right time is crucial to your success! That's why God's wisdom and Spirit are necessary when it comes to planning your schedule. There's a lot that I don't know that He *does* know, so I wouldn't do it without Him. I recommend you do the same. Then, use the following planning strategy:

1. Spend fifteen minutes every evening looking at your dedicated appointments for the next day and upcoming week. Review what's coming up, decide if you need to add or subtract anything, and determine the specific times for those appointments. After that, review your EGT list and goals. (Normally reviewing and modifying my designated checklists becomes an action item on my EGT list.)

2. For approximately thirty minutes every Sunday evening, work on your dedicated appointments, EGT, and goals lists.

3. On the fifteenth of each month, spend about ninety minutes planning the upcoming month. Plan your dedicated appointments, EGT list, goals, and your designated checklists.

4. On the first Wednesday of each calendar quarter, work out a detailed plan for the next twelve months for your dedicated appointments, EGT list, goals, and your designated checklists. This takes me approximately four hours. During this time, I also fill out my "Quarterly Personal Assessment." (See the example on page 146.)

This is so powerful!

Intentionally planning for all *8 Areas* of your life is going to be a wake-up call. You'll start examining your priorities and analyzing your time. Mapping and planning is a simple and realistic process. The simple fact is, time is a commodity. If you're like me, you do not want people wasting it.

Only God knows what your tomorrow looks like. As you plan your time, remember this important point: always align yourself with the wisdom of God, being led by the Spirit. This is crucial to *skillfully* master the art of time management.

Calendar busters add flexibility to the plan.

Here's a true story. One day, I was in a Personal Day of Training (PDOT) with one of my managers. A friend called me up and said he had tickets to a baseball game that day, with seats behind the dugout. Taking him up on that offer meant that I would end the PDOT early. But I decided right then and there I was going to the game. That's called a calendar buster.

I am not bound to my schedule. During the day, if I need to change my schedule for whatever reason, I simply *readjust* and *re-plan*. That's the secret to calendar busters. I'll adjust my scheduled rest or hobbies appointment and re-plan my business appointment. It's an *easy rearrangement* of the schedule. Very simple!

Create a blueprint of the rooms in your life.

At first glance, organizing a system and creating a blueprint for all *8 Areas* of your life can be difficult to comprehend. For starters, maybe you've never seen or acknowledged each of these *8 Areas* in your own life. You might have asked yourself something like, "You mean I have eight areas of my life?" With your next breath, perhaps you commented further saying, "I'm having difficulty with just one area, much less eight."

Focusing on written plans for each area will not only simplify your life, but it will provide you with meaning, purpose, calmness, and direction. At the beginning, though, it will seemingly add more complexity. "Great! I wanted more complexity!" Hang in there. In the long run, with the right plan for each area, you *will* develop a lifestyle you never dreamed possible.

On the following pages, I have shared an example of organizing a blueprint of your dedicated appointments. Notice that under each section of the *8 Areas*, there are "rooms," or specific priorities for which you intend to schedule appointments. Every room has three common features:

1) Each room is a chosen priority.

2) Each room requires a time commitment.

3) Each room will overlap with other rooms.

THE EIGHT AREAS AND ROOMS OF YOUR LIFE

REST PLAN	PLA PLAN	SPIRITUAL PLAN	FUN / HOBBIES PLAN
Relax	Podcasts	Church	Race the Vet
Two Week Vacation	Biographies	Quiet Time	Motorcycle
One Week Vacation	Read	Ministry	Read
Four Day Vacation	Seminars	Bible Study	Football Games
Daily Vacation	Magazines	Weekend Advances	Baseball Games
Walk in the Park	Mentors	Teach / Coach	Do Nothing
Look at the Clouds	School	Serve	Television

THE EIGHT AREAS AND ROOMS OF YOUR LIFE

FAMILY / FRIENDS PLAN	WEALTH PLAN	CAREER / JOB / SCHOOL PLAN	HEALTH PLAN
Date Night With Spouse	Tithe / Seed	Increase Effectiveness	Trainer
Romantic Time With Spouse	Money Management Course	Coach Territories	Aerobics
Time With Adult Children	Investments	Delegate	Body Toning
Grandkids / Friends	Work With Financial Planners	Oversee Systems	Eating Plan
Accountability Time	Estate Planning	Build Territories	Walk
Vacation	Life Insurance	Customers	Sleep
School Events	Will		Physicals

Gigantic ways to create more time in all *8 Areas*:

- ✓ Don't rush past the beginning.
- ✓ Learn the art of politely saying, "No, thank you."
- ✓ View your time as a seed.
- ✓ Meet with the CEO of the world and get God's direction.
- ✓ Treat each day as very important.
- ✓ Practice taking mini-vacations.
- ✓ Never speed when driving.
- ✓ Learn the art of delegation.
- ✓ Don't gossip, argue, or debate.
- ✓ Discipline yourself to get up earlier and go to bed earlier.
- ✓ Exercise a minimum of four times a week.
- ✓ Practice the *15 Healthy Habits*.
- ✓ Look for ways to speak fewer words.
- ✓ Limit how often you check your emails. (Turn off the option for push notifications.)
- ✓ Hire a personal assistant.
- ✓ Declutter your home and workspace.
- ✓ Set maximum time limits on phone calls.
- ✓ Use checklists for all *8 Areas* to keep you focused and efficient. It will make your life easier.
- ✓ Put everything back in its place.
- ✓ Limit the time you watch TV. (This is big!)
- ✓ Limit how long you surf the web.
- ✓ Set time limits for all social media.
- ✓ Don't be in a rush.
- ✓ Don't wait until the last minute to get ready.
- ✓ Use travel time productively.
- ✓ Be cognizant of when people are wasting your time.
- ✓ Read a minimum of four books annually, or even better, read six or seven.
- ✓ Have a mission statement for your life and reanalyze it each quarter.
- ✓ Invest five minutes each day in visualizing the impossible for each of the *8 Areas* of your life (for a total of eight days).
- ✓ Practice self-discipline.

✓ Prepare yourself ahead of time for your meetings.
✓ Leave early for appointments.

As I pointed out earlier, Satan has three goals for your life: to steal, kill, and destroy. One of the primary ways he does this is by robbing you of your time. But today is *the big day* to take it back.

Goal planning made easy: Step One:

Retrain your thinking and paradigms by envisioning the impossible. Get inspired and dream big about your life. What does that look like practically? Write it down! Believe it or not, the Notes app on my smartphone is the tool I find most helpful to me. I recommend using that or something similar.

Simply designate and label one note for each one of the *8 Areas* of your life. Then, write down your impossible dreams for each area. I'm not talking about being silly, but think of something your current paradigm has a hard time comprehending, or better yet, something that may require God's hand to actually produce the manifestation of the dream. Regardless, write down impossible dreams for each of the *8 Areas*.

I'm warning you that this is going to be a tough assignment mentally and physically because it's going to seem like an exercise in futility. Quite the contrary! You're actually retraining your mental muscles to see things differently. It should take no more than an hour to write down several items for all *8 Areas*. Don't try to figure out if the items are "God's will" for your life; just relax and write them down. It's *critically important* that you don't attempt to figure everything out and analyze (and especially overanalyze) any of your dreams.

Change your life in five minutes.

Here comes the fun part. For five minutes each day, get quiet and be still as you pull out your notes and visualize the impossible in only one of the *8 Areas*. Again, take only *five minutes*. At the beginning, you might be sweating bullets and/or feeling like you're living in Fantasyland. However, with due diligence, take one of the *8 Areas* and visualize your dreams for that area. Do this for eight straight days.

Just relax. Close your eyes, and ask God for wisdom. Then start visualizing. Go deep into your spirit. You also may need to set a timer. What you're doing is re-creating your thinking according to the image of God. He will show you great and mighty things in the weeks and months to come. Once again, follow this system every day for eight straight days, repeating the process for the next ninety days or so. You will never be the same again. (By the way, there are times when I've changed my list by either adding or subtracting impossible dreams for one of the *8 Areas*.)

I've also included a form on page 144 called "Above and Beyond" for you to see as an example. Feel free to use it and write down some dreams there.

What's happening to your subconscious?

Your thinking, as well as what and how you see, will start to change slowly and methodically. This is not self-hypnosis. This is retraining your paradigms and detoxing them of all the junk you've been trained to believe for many years. The blinders over your eyes will simply start falling away. It's a process. After practicing this for about sixty to ninety days, you'll feel like you're seeing into the "promised land" of your life.

Having shared all this, in order for it to work properly, four significant details must be in place:

1. All the above needs to be accompanied with a ferocious Powerful Learning Agenda (PLA). We cover this in greater detail in Chapter 16.
2. In everything, you must also intentionally align yourself with the wisdom and Spirit of God, and practice developing your faith.
3. You need to know where you are today regarding your goals. To help with this, I've included a "Quarterly Personal Assessment" on page 146. This needs to be

filled out once a quarter so you can strategically and consistently track your growth.

4. You need to develop a practical process for your goal planning, which is Step Two.

Goal planning made easy: Step Two:

Implement a blueprint of your goals. This step is simple and practical.

Take one thing you can do to improve your life (for example, a dream from the "Above and Beyond" form that you'll fill out), being careful not to overcomplicate your goal. Again, choose only *one thing* in each of the *8 Areas*, and create a blueprint of them as shown on "Blueprint Contract" found on page 145. To help you stay accountable, I strongly encourage you to use this form. It's like having a contract with yourself. Be sure to sign it.

Then, once a week, take fifteen minutes (preferably on Sunday evening or your day off, depending on your schedule) and review your one item for all *8 Areas*.

When you complete an item for one of the *8 Areas*, take a red felt-tip pen and write *Complete* (with the date) across the top of the contract in big letters, then place it on your mirror where you can see it each day. Afterward, write up another contract adding a new item for that area of your life.

You were designed to be visionary *and* practical.

The practical application of goal planning and blueprinting and the visionary application of taking five minutes a day to envision the impossible can seem contradictory or even like opposites. Some intellectual people have a hard time visualizing the impossible because, when you're practical and science-oriented, it seems illogical to envision the impossible, or it could even sound like you're making up fairy tales. On the other hand, people who are more visionary have a hard time with the practicality of writing down dreams and blueprints and actually *planning* goals.

What I'm talking about is bringing the practical and the visionary applications together. You're connecting the two by retraining both the visual and the psychological sides. *In fact, what you're really connecting is the spiritual **and** the natural.*

Most people are visual and remember with pictures, so in addition to all that, what you're doing is changing the picture (the vision) you have in your mind about each area of your life. Being visionary and practical is not contradictory. The fact is, you were designed to be both!

THE BIG DAY

Above and Beyond

Year:

_____

Area:

_____

1. _____

2. _____

3. _____

4. _____

5. _____

6. _____

7. _____

8. _____

9. _____

10. _____

THE BIG DAY
Blueprint Contract

THE GOAL: _____

What is important to you about this goal? _____

_____

List one person who knows about this goal: _____

List the obstacles: _____

_____

Describe in detail the steps for reaching this goal: _____

_____

I, _____, as of this date, _____, do promise to give myself to do everything at my disposal to achieve this goal set before me. It is my choice to commit effort, discipline, and planning to achieve this goal. I will achieve this goal no later than _____, and my signature is my word that this goal will be completed no later than this date.

Signature: _____ Date: _____

QUARTERLY PERSONAL ASSESSMENT

_____ QUARTER OF THE YEAR 20 _____

Evaluate yourself in the *8 Areas* of your life using the following grading system:

A = Performing at peak levels / going "above and beyond"
B = Doing a satisfactory or good job / accomplishing what needs to be done but not more than that
C = Average, simply going through the motions / maintaining
D = Failing at this time

Now, before starting this exercise — especially for the first time — recognize that you are currently in one of three phases in every area of your life: the beginning, the intermediate, or the mature. Choose the phase you believe you are currently in for each area, and then grade yourself on that area.

Area of Your Life	Current Phase	Grade
Spiritual		
Health		
Family/Friends		
Career/Job/School		
Financial		
PLA		
Rest		
Hobby/Fun		

Keynotes:

- Your plan consists of three areas: your appointments, your to-do lists, and your goals.
- The problem is not a lack of time on any given day; it's simply the lack of an effective time management system with disciplined implementation.
- Without the plan, the alignments get lost in ineffective time management.
- Learn "The Big Day Time Management System": SEE IT – PLAN IT – DO IT – EXPECT IT – REPLAN IT.
- Your God-given destiny is to experience greatness and fulfillment in all *8 Areas* simultaneously, with each one operating effectively.
- Setting up a system for managing your time involves four areas of mapping out your time and four areas of planning your goals.
- You are not bound by your schedule. If you run into a calendar buster, then simply readjust and re-plan the schedule.
- Create a blueprint for your priorities, otherwise known as the "rooms of your life."
- There are two easy steps to goal planning: 1) envision the impossible, and 2) implement a blueprint for what you envision.
- To help with planning your goals, utilize the following forms: "Above and Beyond," "Blueprint Contract," and the "Quarterly Personal Assessment."
- Bringing the practical and visionary applications together is actually connecting the spiritual and the natural.

CHAPTER SIXTEEN

Cornerstone 3 – Your Thinking

One of the top three areas we need to work on the most is how we think and what we speak. The way we think, or the way we personally see things and what we believe, is reflected in the words we speak.

We live in a fear-based society, which teaches us to verbalize words over our own lives and others that are actually detrimental. Then we justify ourselves by saying we're "just being honest" or "just joking." What we are really doing is rehearsing the junk over and over.

Our thoughts and our words have tremendous power. The key is to simply harness our thought life and the words we speak. Another way to say that is to detox all the junk that's unproductive and fear-based. I'm not talking about being positive. I'm talking about being realistic, which is simply a matter of taking the problem and turning it into an opportunity.

To repair the problem, we must come up with steps and a process. We don't just say, "Oh, it will turn out OK." Once we have our process, we move forward in a calm and articulate way.

Regardless of whether you believe it or not, you will attract exactly what you expect and what you say. It's the law of attraction. To say it even better, it's the law of the spiritual and the law of the natural at work before your very eyes. Retraining your thinking and your words is not magical or automatic. It comes through a consistency of good habits, even (and sometimes especially) in the midst of the junkyards of life.

Think about what you're thinking about. (Read that sentence again if you need to.) Don't have a mouth that runs two hundred miles per hour and a brain that runs twenty miles per hour. *Think* about what you're saying. To retrain your words, you must retrain your thinking first.

What you believe becomes your reality.

Often, what we believe is only our opinion, or even better, the opinions of others who hold the mainstream views of the world. One of those predominant views is that average is OK. Is it really?

The Bible says, "Do not conform to the pattern of this world, but be transformed by the renewing of your mind."[61] Renewed by what? The mind of Christ. "But we have the mind of Christ [to be guided by His thoughts and purposes]."[62]

You are what you think. Today, start changing your thinking from average to great. The most practical way to change your thinking is to develop a powerful learning agenda.

Change your thinking with a Powerful Learning Agenda.

The reason for introducing you to a PLA is to get you to think differently, to break through your current paradigms and reshape them, and to retrain you to think higher thoughts. In other words, it's about your mind being renewed until you've learned how to *skillfully master the art of living according to God's standards in all 8 Areas of your life*. That's the purpose of a PLA.

Also note that the keyword here is *skillfully*. It requires wisdom to master the art of living. Living the abundant life and mastering our skill sets in every area is like mastering the skill of playing an instrument. Most of us don't see it that way though. We don't think of our life as an instrument. We just treat every day like a normal day when we get up. But *the big day* is all about using *today* to shift that paradigm and retrain your thinking.

What you think about is what you are. It's just that simple. And everything you believe right now is because of what you've been trained to believe. We've been trained by well-meaning coaches, pastors, books, seminars, parents, teachers, advertisers, the stigma of "keeping up with the Joneses," as well as both good and bad experiences. The list goes on and on.

Have you stopped to consider what and who is training your thinking, or why you think about the things you think about? That's what your PLA is for: to set the highest standard of influence over your thinking so that you can be skilled in every area of your life and master the art of living abundantly.

The *A* in PLA stands for *Agenda*. This is like a checklist of what you're going to do and what will help you reshape your paradigms. It can include reading and studying the Bible, as well as getting involved with a great community, church, and/or other smaller groups like Bible studies. This checklist can also consist of activities like listening to Christian songs, watching inspiring movies and shows, reading great books, and utilizing electronic media as a resource for hundreds of gifted teachers. (Remember, this is not about being religious — just the opposite. It's about combining the spiritual and natural arenas of life.)

The Holy Spirit can also be a part of your PLA. The Holy Spirit's anointing is not just for Sunday. It's there for you when you get out of bed Monday through Saturday. It's there for you when you build multiple streams of income. It's there for your relationships. It's there for you when you want to increase the level of your health and fitness. The Holy Spirit is there for you every day to help you master every area of your life!

The fact that you have help every day is encouraging because your PLA is a process, and skillfully mastering life is also a process. As an example, just because you love God does not mean you've "arrived" and have no room for further growth in your relationship with Him. No! You can grow more in that area just as you can grow more in every area of your life. But there's a *process* that you need to set in place in order to master each area. That's why you have a PLA.

To make it even better, when you learn to skillfully master each area, it adds credibility and growth to other areas. For example,

I have purposefully retrained my thinking and mastered the skill of not debating or arguing with others. This strengthens me in relationships, which enriches me in the area of business and adds to my health as well.

In other words, your PLA significantly increases your skillfulness in the art of winning big.

Today is *the big day — to change your thinking*!

Here's a bonus tip.

Make the most out of your car or other means of transportation. Turn it into "Vehicle University." Have audiobooks or teachings ready to go every time you travel somewhere. Also, you should purposely read for thirty minutes each day.

Spend time developing the shift from average to great, beginning on the inside. Change happens on the inside first, and it inevitably manifests on the outside. Your life will change before your very eyes when you change your thinking!

Keynotes:

- Go to work on your thinking with a Powerful Learning Agenda (PLA).
- Think about what you're thinking about.
- Don't have a mouth that runs two hundred miles per hour and a brain that runs twenty miles per hour.
- What you believe becomes your reality.
- Don't conform to the patterns of this world.
- Practice skillfully mastering the art of living according to God's standards in all *8 Areas* of your life. That's the purpose of a PLA.
- What you think about is what you are.
- The Holy Spirit can also be a part of your PLA.
- Make the most out of your car or other means of transportation by turning it into "Vehicle University."
- Purposely read for thirty minutes each day.

CHAPTER SEVENTEEN

Cornerstone 4 – Your Disciplines

After your alignments, your plan, and your thinking (and PLA), the next most important cornerstone is all about your disciplines. When you practice a disciplined lifestyle in all *8 Areas*, when you do the small things right every day, not only does it add a multitude of benefits to your life, but you'll truly experience what it means to *win big*, to live a full life. It is imperative to our success that we make a conscious decision to practice discipline every single day. Having zero or no discipline produces an average or below-average life.

See yourself as a disciplined individual.

Seeing yourself as having self-discipline is the starting point, especially when you don't feel like it. Self-control is a fruit of the Spirit, and one of the results is self-discipline. Your choices produce the consequences. Your thoughts produce your choices. Every day, you should declare over yourself, "I am a disciplined person, and I make wise choices." That is powerful.

Training your thoughts and your words are the two top disciplines.

We've covered it before, but it bears repeating. Discipline yourself in what you think about. Discipline your thought life. Purposefully choose to dwell on great, life-giving thoughts. The Bible even tells us what to think about. It's literally a checklist:

"Finally, believers, whatever is true, whatever is honorable and worthy of respect, whatever is right and confirmed by God's word, whatever is pure and wholesome, whatever is lovely and brings peace, whatever is admirable and of good repute; if there is any excellence, if there is anything worthy of praise, think continually on these things [center your mind on them, and implant them in your heart]."[63]

The second most important discipline has to do with the words you speak. Train yourself to remove the junk from your vocabulary. I'm not only talking about cuss words. I'm talking about speaking death over yourself and others. Be aware of what you're saying. Your words are seeds. They are powerful. Describing the power of words, the Bible says that "the power of life and death is in the tongue."[64]

Build a disciplined lifestyle.

- Ask God to help you.
- Prophesy over yourself. Every day, speak over yourself, "I am a disciplined person."
- *See* yourself as a disciplined person. Envision it. This is critically important.
- Comprehend the reality that without pain you will have no growth. Embrace the pain.
- Start one discipline each month. Only one — not ten, not five, not even two. Just one a month. This one discipline will give you confidence in many ways and avenues.
- Have a plan for what you're going to do regarding that one discipline. Write out the action plan.
- Be accountable to others for that one discipline. Have someone with whom you can stay accountable daily or weekly via email or text.
- Remember, one of God's favorite words is *practice*. What you're doing is practicing that one discipline each day. Don't give up hope if you fail. Just keep practicing.
- Take the first step and just do it — today. One day at a time. Today is your *big day.*

Remember that what you're doing is *training*. Training your thought life. Training your words. Training your choices. Training yourself to say, "No, thank you." Training yourself to be diligent. Training yourself to be uncomfortable. Training yourself to be grateful. Training yourself to walk in the peace of God. Training yourself not to worry or fret. Training yourself to see the best in people. Training yourself to walk in the wisdom of God. Training yourself to allow God's words to work through your life.

In each of these ways you train yourself, you will also become an example for others. You will become a "light on the hill" when others see your disciplined actions. You will inspire others!

Great, disciplined choices equal great habits.

I have heard it said that it takes seventy-five to ninety days to form a habit. During that time, what I'm doing is developing disciplines which then form habits. If we have bad habits, it means we have trained ourselves one step at a time to make poor choices. Making bad choices ends *today*!

What are the striking benefits of a disciplined life? I've listed nineteen below.

- There is purpose in all that you do each day.
- You know which direction to go and which steps to take.
- You have peace even in the midst of a storm.
- This gives you confidence that, through Christ, there is nothing you cannot do.
- Discipline will produce incredible blessings from God in your life.
- You will see an abundance of greatness in all *8 Areas*.
- Discipline will help produce the fruit of the Spirit: love, joy, peace, patience, kindness, goodness, faithfulness, gentleness, and self-control.[65]
- Discipline will turn your dreams into reality.
- Discipline allows you to have a healthy lifestyle along with an effective exercise program.
- Discipline will give you the freedom of choice and the freedom to have a life of fulfillment.
- The benefits of discipline will put you in a position to be "in a position."
- Discipline will always put the odds in your favor.

- Your life will be a light on the hill for all to see.
- Discipline keeps you from wasting time.
- Being disciplined will attract other disciplined people into your life, which will further motivate you.
- Discipline transitions you from being conformed to this world to being transformed by God.
- Discipline helps you avoid following the crowd.
- The combined benefits of a disciplined life will help you reach your high calling.
- Bottom line: discipline helps you tame your feelings and emotions.

Keynotes:

- See yourself as a disciplined individual.
- Self-control is a fruit of the Spirit, and one of the results is self-discipline.
- Discipline your thought life and the words you speak.
- Your words are seeds.
- Discipline is about training.
- Great, disciplined choices equal great habits.
- Discipline will always put the odds in your favor.

CHAPTER EIGHTEEN

Cornerstone 5 — Your Attitude

Your attitude affects everything, from the start of your day to how your day progresses. The issue is not that it's good or bad "out there" — it is either good or bad in *you*. Change your attitude to "Yes, this is my big day!" and then you'll find the birds singing louder and the grass looking greener.

Your attitude is either an asset or a liability. Your attitude affects events, relationships, sales, the growth of your business, etc. A positive attitude will give you the strength to climb the mountain, but a negative attitude will cause you to focus on the problem.

Your attitude determines your reality and how you see the world. We are not talking about being Pollyanna, saying "Oh, don't worry. Everything is going to be OK!" but seeing reality as it really is so that you know how to approach it. Attitude is a vehicle that drives you to either an average life or one that's above and beyond. Today is your *big day* to make the quality decision to practice developing your attitude.

I am not positive for the sake of being positive.

I would rather you cuss me out than tell me I'm an optimist. Truth is, I am just a realistic person looking at the facts and analyzing the details of a situation. But I *am* determined to develop my faith in every situation. I want faith to construct my reality for today and my future. This attitude positions me to find an answer versus focusing on the problem, which in turn gives me a better chance of discovering practical solutions to everyday problems.

Remember, we no longer call problems *problems* but opportunities. This paradigm gives me a spirit of calmness in the midst of a storm. If you're calm and collected, it makes sense

161

that you would be able to look at things much more objectively. By the way, I'm not saying that I look for the easy solution. I'm looking for solutions that will stand the test of time. Sometimes that does take time. (Once again, don't rush past the beginning.)

Don't chase the stuff.

The richest man in the Bible did not chase stuff. He pursued the wisdom of God. That's what he sought more than anything. That's what he desired. He exemplified an attitude contrary to what we are so often taught. The world systems teach us to get, get, get. The Bible teaches us to give, give, give.

I'm not teaching you to be poor. Quite the contrary! I'm teaching you to change your attitude because "with God, all things are possible."[66] Wow! Notice the operative words: "with God." *With God,* you get an abundant life.

The Bible gives us Jesus's instruction to "seek first His kingdom and His righteousness, and all these things will be added to you."[67] Learning the ways of God (like giving) propels you into supernatural abundance. You don't have to chase the stuff to get the stuff, but if you pursue God and the principles He gives us, then there is always a great reward. Your attitude makes all the difference because your attitude will determine your focus.

My love for money directed my attitude about life.

I grew up with an affluent lifestyle. Living on two acres and keeping a full-time maid are just a couple of examples of how we lacked nothing. When I realized what money could do, there was no doubt about it: I worshiped money. I coveted money — lots of money.

I started my first business when I was eleven years old. Did I say how much I loved money? Then God turned my light on, and I saw that money was nothing but a tool, just like my cell phone or my car, and just like the chair I'm sitting in. You get the point. That's when my life started to change for the better. The result? I no longer worshiped the tools. Don't get me wrong: I love nice tools; there's so much you can do with them.

But my attitude about them affects the rest of my life, which is crucial to understand.

Stay focused on the right things.

Focusing on the wrong things will have a major, negative effect on your attitude. Feeling depressed, confused, or sorry for yourself, or feeling like your world is upside down for no apparent reason are symptoms of not having the right attitude and mental focus. The good news is, God has a wonderful plan for every day of your life, including today, *the big day*. Get refocused and practice developing a higher perspective:

"Therefore if you have been raised with Christ [to a new life, sharing in His resurrection from the dead], keep seeking the things that are above, where Christ is, seated at the right hand of God. Set your mind and keep focused habitually on the things above [the heavenly things], not on things that are on the earth [which have only temporal value]."[68]

Wise people like to be corrected.

One of the purposes of the Bible is to give instruction regarding our attitude and our perspectives. Wise people like being corrected because they love learning a better way. (Contrary to Mr. I-Know-That, also known as Mr. Prima Donna!) One of my goals is to change the direction of the way I'm doing things so that I'm more effective and efficient, and yes, that does mean change. This is going to sound tough, but it's true: when you're full of yourself and you never like to be corrected, you have aligned yourself with the characteristics of a fool. (Wow, that is so strong!)

Review the first five cornerstones.

Again, the first five cornerstones make up the vehicle which determines the way your life is naturally progressing. Remember the goals we started talking about in previous chapters? That's where you're headed in life. Your alignments, plan, thinking, disciplines, and attitude are each a part of the

163

vehicle that gets you to the attainment of your goals in all *8 Areas* of your life. Cornerstones 6–11 are the fuel for your vehicle. Let's discuss that now.

Keynotes:

- Your attitude affects everything in your life.
- A positive attitude gives you strength to face the opportunities life throws at you.
- A negative attitude will cause you to focus on the problem.
- The world systems teach us to get, get, get. The Bible teaches us to give, give, give.
- We have to realize money is a tool, not a god.
- God has a wonderful plan for your life.
- Wise people like to be corrected because they love learning a better way.

CHAPTER NINETEEN

Cornerstone 6 — Your Systems

Your systems will produce operational excellence for your professional life as well as your personal life. Systems will also establish a platform for growth and improvement in everything from time management to higher profits. Systems are teachable, and therefore, reproducible. With correct systems, you will have more income and fewer costs, as well as a more effective way of accomplishing tasks from A to Z.

One of the best examples is the Pareto Principle, also known as the 80/20 Rule, which states that 80 percent of effects come from 20 percent of the cause, or, in other words, 20 percent of what you invest produces 80 percent of the results. Systems give you a way of raising the cause (input), which, in turn, raises effectiveness (results). Today is your *big day* to develop systems that produce positive results in every area of your life and business.

Systems produce operational excellence.

You can produce systems for all *8 Areas* of your life. I know that may sound foreign and even strange, but the reality is that we have not been well-trained to apply systems in our everyday life. But, this entire book has been written with a systematic approach so that you can use it as a tool for improving your overall effectiveness.

We are going to break it down to its simplest form. Let's start by defining what a system really is:

1. "an assemblage or combination of   things   or   parts forming a complex or unitary whole

2. a coordinated body of methods or a scheme or plan of procedure; organizational scheme

3. any formulated, regular, or special method or plan of procedure"[69]

Basically, it's a structure. Now, don't let this sound like it's only for an engineer or a NASA control center. In reality, systems should be a basic part of our everyday life. The key is knowing how to utilize these structures and make the most of their potential.

What is the purpose of a system?

How would you like to have consistent, predictable results day in and day out? Sounds good to me! Let's break it down like this. Let's consider one area of your life, like your wealth plan, although we could use any area as an example.

Your wealth plan is not based on how much money you make but what you do with what you have left over each month. Do you know what the purpose of a budget is? Its primary purpose is to help you build wealth. It's a *system*. See how simple that is?

What is the purpose of a great health plan? It produces the predictable results of better health. This is not rocket science. This is simply implementing a process or procedure that puts the odds in your favor for a predictable outcome. At the beginning of the book, we talked about winning big — real big. The secret weapon of winning real big in all *8 Areas* of your life is simply the disciplined implementation of a system that raises the odds of your success.

Systems developed the "Odds Capital" of the world.

Las Vegas is called the "Odds Capital" of the world because the house wins most the time. Why? The odds are in their favor. If you think you can beat the odds, think again. Because of the house edge (the odds), the casino will always win in the long run, no matter how smart you are or how smart you think you are. Quite simply, that's the way life is.

A system built correctly can put the odds in *your* favor in any area of your life. However, not having a system is called gambling. If you don't have a system for the areas of your life, you're actually gambling with your life! Once again, if you *do* have a system, you have just raised the odds of your success. You have put the odds in your favor.

Having said all this, know that a system is not perfect. It's not intended to be perfect. It's simply designed to raise the odds in your favor. In addition, removing pressure is another beneficial result of implementing a system.

Systems establish a platform for growth.

As you develop systems in the *8 Areas* of your life, you will begin to see a growth that is trackable and predictable most of the time. Think of your health: the more calories that go in versus those that go out means expanse. That's trackable and predictable.

The good news is, you do not need to reinvent the wheel for a great system. Many efficient systems have been provided throughout this book. You will find them listed below. Your job is to practice what's in the book. Practice the checklists repeatedly, and establish the systems and structures so that you set a solid foundation for trackable, predictable growth in every area. Don't let these overwhelm you. First, review them, and then take it one step at a time. Here we go:

1. Build a Keynote Book with eight different sections.
2. Use "Wisdom's Checklist of the Past" on page 61.
3. Practice focusing on living in the right time zone.
4. When your world turns upside down, bring out "The Big Guns" checklist on page 75.
5. Review the ingredients of a bad decision on pages 77-78 and practice avoiding them.
6. Review the ingredients of a wise decision on pages 78-79 and start practicing them.

7. Review the "5 Most Important Questions" to ask yourself each day on page 85-86, and practice asking yourself these questions daily.
8. Review the list of affirmations on pages 86-88. Develop your personal list of affirmations, and practice speaking them over yourself.
9. Practice using the *15 Healthy Habits* on page 91.
10. Practice using the "Decision-Making Checklist" (for the three types of decisions) on pages 98-100.
11. Build your wise counsel board.
12. Practice the points on "The Power of Letting Go" checklist on page 107.
13. Review the *11 Cornerstones* on page 112. Cornerstones 1–5 are your vehicle, or the way your life is progressing. Practice developing the condition of this vehicle. Add the fuel of Cornerstones 6–11 to your vehicle.
14. Review the Top 15 Excuses on page 120 and remove them from your vocabulary.
15. Practice aligning yourself with the Top 10 Spiritual Alignments on pages 121-125.
16. Change your thinking: develop a ferocious Powerful Learning Agenda (PLA), creating and implementing dedicated appointments for what you put on your list.
17. Practice effective time management: map out the *8 Areas* of your life according to the four areas listed on pages 132-134.
18. Start scheduling your dedicated appointments.
19. Start developing your Expect Great Things (EGT) list.
20. Implement the four areas of time planning found on pages 134-135.
21. Practice the "Gigantic ways to create more time in all *8 Areas*" listed on page 139.
22. Use the "Above and Beyond" goal plan on page 144.
23. Use the "Blueprint Contract" goal plan on page 145.
24. Track your growth by using the "Quarterly Personal Assessment" on page 146.

25. Remind yourself of the benefits of a disciplined life found on pages 157-158.

Raise the bar of excellence.

I believe you will see a significant improvement in all *8 Areas* of your life if you start practicing the systems and checklists laid before you today.

Note: I did not say your life would be perfect. I am not guaranteeing your success. This is not about sudden perfection or swallowing a magic pill. It's about you making a decision *today* to advance your life and develop who you are, starting wherever you are now, no matter where you've been.

Now, you can decide to raise the bar of excellence in your life today, but keep in mind that the *quality* of that decision matters greatly. You will need to decide if you're going to bring your A-Game, B-Game, C-Game, or D-Game. What do I mean?

- A-Game: working diligently every day; displaying the characteristics of a warrior and a champion.
- B-Game: working well, with a hit or miss every now and then.
- C-Game: being sloppy and lazy; average at best.
- D-Game: failing; lazy and lethargic; or not trying.

The quality of your decision is 100 percent your choice. It's not God's choice. It's neither your spouse's choice nor your boss's choice. It's *your* choice. It's going to take work, dedication, discipline, focus, planning, failing, being uncomfortable, and lots of practice, practice, and more practice.

No matter which game you bring today, I encourage you to always see yourself as someone who brings their A-Game. Shoot for that. Raise the bar. Even if you don't see overnight results, don't let that limit you or your perspective of yourself to anything less than the best. You're made in "God-class." In other words, you're made in God's image. It's like being state-of-the-art or top-of-the-line. That means *you* are someone who *can* bring their A-Game every time and win.

As you implement and practice these and other systems, remember they aren't meant to produce overnight perfection in every area of your life. Sometimes you won't even experience instant results. However, over time and with consistency, you will see incredible results. You will experience firsthand how systems raise the odds of your success.

Are you ready to win big? Today is the day!

Keynotes:

- Your systems will produce operational excellence.
- Systems will also produce a platform of trackable and predictable growth.
- Systems are teachable and reproducible.
- Systems are basic to everyday life.
- *The Big Day* consists of both natural and spiritual systems, concepts, and ideas.
- A system is a set of principles that produces an organized method of results.
- Systems don't work for you by happenstance. You have to work a system in order to make it work for you.
- Systems are not perfect.
- The good news is, you don't need to reinvent the wheel.
- Practice the twenty-five systems in *The Big Day* that put the odds in your favor.
- It's your choice whether you bring your A-Game, B-Game, C-Game, or D-game.
- You're state-of-the-art, top-of-the-line—someone made in "God-class."

CHAPTER TWENTY

Cornerstone 7 — Your Resolve

Shed *pansy-itis*! Starting today, remove the phrase "It's hard" from your vocabulary. Resolve to replace the word *problem* with *opportunity*.

It's a fact that stuff happens to all of us. However, it's what we do with that stuff that determines what will become of us. That problem, obstacle, or mountain can be the very thing that catapults your life into greatness. It could bring you to your greatest hour. How determined are you to see that happen? It's up to the level of your resolve!

Sadly, we live in a society that is well-trained to pursue instant gratification and entitlements, so oftentimes we're found wanting in the area of resolve. We don't have the strength or courage to stick it out and press through for the best results.

Moreover, when you come upon an opportunity, two of the devil's favorite sayings are "It's over" and "You're finished." He's attempting to get you to agree with him by means of worry and fear. Worry and fear are two of the most negative emotions we can experience, and neither of them actually enables us to overcome the opportunity we're facing. In fact, worry and fear will zap all our strength and resolve if we let them. What then should we do?

The Bible says it best: "God cares for you, so turn all your worries over to him."[70] It is *not* over when we face an opportunity — we don't play a nine-inning game. We play until we *win*! Put a smile on your face and in your heart, and "go get 'em!" Stay determined to be strong and courageous! Seize every opportunity with greatness and resolve.

Beware: the road is out.

As you read earlier, the first five cornerstones represent your vehicle, and Cornerstones 6–11 represent the fuel that you choose to put in your vehicle. In most cases, we have a choice when it comes to which vehicle we use on our journey of life.

But what happens to our journey when the road is washed out? How do we respond when the road is filled with potholes or covered in ice? What if a storm is raging or we're faced with other negative situations beyond our control? Other scenarios include detours, demons, challenging people, financial reversals, sickness, loss of a loved one, bankruptcy, and divorce—the list goes on and on.

Fact: we are all going to face adversity—some major, some minor, and some in between—but whichever kind it is, the level of intensity is determined by our world, circumstances, and perception. It's relative to us personally. What I mean is, a situation may not be hard for one person, but for another, it could be extremely challenging. The obstacles in the road may keep one person from moving forward, but others may find their way around them.

Who wants to travel on Pansy-itis Airlines?

We have been trained to be led by our inner feelings when we face adversity. Not only that, but we've been trained by the world around us to follow the crowd to the airport and join them as a passenger on Pansy-itis Airlines.

Like everyone else, the ticket agent meets you and hands you some tissues for your tears. Stamped on your ticket, you see the words, "It's OK to give up and be average. You weren't meant to achieve your goals." If that weren't enough, you also read what's written under that in bold, red, capital letters: "God is mad at you and it's too late. It's over and it's finished."

As you board the plane, you notice another crew member addressing each passenger with the same defeated words. "Life is just so tough, isn't it? After all, it's not your fault," he says with a sad countenance. You notice on the other side of your ticket it says, "Don't worry. The government is going to take care of everything." Squinting, you notice the fine print at the bottom of the ticket: "Look for a job with great benefits. This is your only hope."

Will you choose to settle in?

As you take your seat, they offer you free shots of alcohol to ease your pain as well as coloring books to help you get in touch with your emotions. If you don't drink, they have your favorite prescription on hand, since, of course, the answer is just one pill away. Yes, everything is free.

As you settle into your comfortable seat, you notice they also have free movies. You have three choices: 1) How to Devise 10 Excuses for Staying Average, 2) Why Being Disciplined Is Overrated, and 3) Living in the Past: The Good Ol' Days.

You also can't help but observe how everyone on the airplane looks miserable and dejected, almost resembling zombies. Over the loudspeaker, you hear a flight attendant giving the last call: "This is your last chance to exit Pansy-itis Airlines."

You suddenly can't help it; you've absolutely had enough of this awful environment! You make a break for it and exit the plane with a sense of newfound freedom and opportunity ahead of you. You choose to believe that today is *the big day* for a new start. How relieving and exhilarating it feels! All your prior excuses disappear, and you no longer feel sorry for yourself. That's when you notice another airline at the gate right across from you.

Warrior Airlines will take your farther.

You start to investigate this new airline. Enthusiastic and lively, the ticket agent has a big smile, is very courteous, and wants to serve you by answering any questions you have. It doesn't take long before you decide to purchase a ticket. (Great first step!)

Written on the ticket, you see the words, "This is your big day. With God, all things are possible!" On the other side of the ticket you read, "You are on your way to your promised land. It's going to take a lot of work, dedication, perseverance, training, and discipline. Start with a strong PLA." It makes perfect sense. The land of opportunity awaits.

Boarding the plane, the welcoming flight attendant asks if you would like a good book to read for the journey, adding that, "There are many stories of those who flew with us to the promised land." You recognize one of the books of the Bible: 2 Corinthians. Flipping through, you become captivated by the story of the apostle Paul. Talk about great adversity! You're inspired by his bulldog faith and never-give-up resolve.

Let Paul's testimony inspire you.

> Are they [self-proclaimed] servants of Christ — I am speaking as if I were out of my mind — I am more so [for I exceed them]; with far more labors, with far more imprisonments, beaten times without number, and often in danger of death. Five times I received from the Jews thirty-nine lashes. Three times I was beaten with rods, once I was stoned. Three times I was shipwrecked, a night and a day I have spent adrift on the sea; many times on journeys, [exposed to] danger from rivers, danger from bandits, danger from my own countrymen, danger from the Gentiles, danger in the city, danger in the wilderness, danger on the sea, danger among those posing as believers; in labor and hardship, often unable to sleep, in hunger and thirst, often [driven to] fasting [for lack of food], in cold and exposure [without adequate clothing].[71]

Wow! You wonder how he made it through all of that. Moved by his story, you continue to the next chapter. The answer to your question suddenly leaps off the page when you read the words of God as He responded to Paul saying, "My grace is sufficient for you [My lovingkindness and My mercy are more than enough—always available—regardless of the situation]; for [My] power is being perfected [and is completed and shows itself most effectively] in [your] weakness."[72] You realize that it's God's grace and power working in you too, and you're ready to fly.

Shake it off.

One morning, when I was feeling sorry for myself, complaining and moaning about the many problems I was facing, my gorgeous wife said, "I want you to listen to something." Now brace yourself. Nancy wanted me to listen to the song "Shake It Off" by Taylor Swift.

I honestly thought it was the dumbest thing I'd ever seen or heard. Taylor Swift started singing, and my wife ordered me, "Now, shake it off!" I told her there was absolutely no way. She responded all the more emphatically, "Yes, dance and shake it off!" For the sake of amusing her, I did.

I thought I looked so stupid and ridiculous. As I continued to "shake it off," something happened on the inside. I started feeling the cares of this world fall off me. The more I shook, the more they faded away. We started dancing and laughing, and as God is my witness, within three minutes I did not have a care in the world. True story! I dare you to try it next time you have an opportunity to do so. In fact, try it for the next three months. You'll notice a difference as well!

Be resolved to conquer the giants in the land.

As you progress and grow, I guarantee that you will face all types of "giants" in your life. Every great story, every great purpose, and every great person experienced tremendous opposition.

In any sport, a game without the defense trying to stop the offense would be a very dull game. One of the greatest games of all time, as far as overcoming adversity, is one that I witnessed: the 2016 Alamo Bowl game between Oregon and TCU. By halftime, the score was Oregon 31 and TCU 0. In one of the most exciting comebacks in collegiate football history, TCU came back to beat Oregon 47–41 in triple overtime. It was unbelievably thrilling to have been at this event! And what about Super Bowl 51 when New England came back to defeat Atlanta?!

That's the reality of what we're facing each day. Most of us have never been trained, let alone well-equipped to go for the gold medal in our life, especially when it's what others may see as a "major comeback." Whatever that gold medal represents in any of the *8 Areas* of your life, it's time to know how to defeat the giants that stand in the way. This is going to take resolve — deliberate resolve every single day.

As you begin to perfect your skills in every area, you will see the giants fall one at a time. You may even look around one day, noticing that certain things are easier than before, and you'll realize that those giants and oppositions disappeared without you even realizing it.

This book is designed to equip you to defeat the giants you face every day. My mother once encouraged me to "hit the bully in the stomach." I will never forget what I learned from that. Stop being intimidated by the giants. Embrace this day with bulldog faith, positioning yourself to never ever, ever, ever give up. No matter what you face. No matter how big the obstacle. God, the greater One, lives on the inside of you.[73] Again, you're made in God's image. Remember who you are and who is with you when you take on the giants in the land.

Combine the wisdom of God, adversity, and bulldog faith.

I would encourage you to research top comebacks from entrepreneurs to Fortune 500 companies to influential individuals. Truth is, we were all designed to have a drive in us to go for our high calling.

How can you make the most out of *the big day*? One big way is to view adversity, whether large or small, as the very thing that can catapult you above and beyond.

The Bible is clear about how adversity, coupled with bulldog faith, can catapult you into greatness. Read the following verses carefully. Observe the role of God's wisdom during adversity and ask Him for it.

> Consider it nothing but joy, my brothers and sisters, whenever you fall into various trials. Be assured that the testing of your faith [through experience] produces endurance [leading to spiritual maturity, and inner peace]. And let endurance have its perfect result and do a thorough work, so that you may be perfect and completely developed [in your faith], lacking in nothing.

> If any of you lacks wisdom [to guide him through a decision or circumstance], he is to ask of [our benevolent] God, who gives to everyone generously and without rebuke or blame, and it will be given to him. But he must ask [for wisdom] in faith, without doubting [God's willingness to help].[74]

What are some ways to make good decisions in the midst of adversity?

Here is my checklist for the "Top 18 Ways to Handle Adversity." This goes for most types of adversity but not necessarily all of them. Remember once again, problems and adversity are now called *opportunities*.

1. Ask God for wisdom to solve the opportunity. Speak life over the opportunity. Don't rehearse the problem over and over.
2. Don't look for an easy fix. Don't be in a rush to get a quick solution just so you don't have to think about it anymore. You want a real solution, not a Band-Aid.
3. Be calm and collected, not emotionally too high or low. Be relaxed and at peace.
4. Put together a plan of action. Also, come up with Plan B and Plan C.

5. Ask God to help you. This sounds so simplistic, but you must realize that you were not designed to *be* God, so stop acting like you were. You're not God, but He is there to help you. Just ask and receive.

6. Evaluate the root of the opportunity. Be very honest with yourself. Address it analytically and objectively.

7. Set realistic expectations of solutions and time frames.

8. Switch or change your perspective. Don't look at it the same way but approach it from another angle.

9. Don't let the problem (opportunity) harass you. Most importantly, do not bring it to the dinner table or to bed. This is critical.

10. Set a dedicated appointment for focusing on that opportunity. Don't think about it again until then. If you need to set a second, third, or fourth appointment, then go ahead.

11. Don't let the adversity define who you are.

12. Forgive yourself and anyone else involved. Don't be critical, judgmental, or condemning toward yourself and others. Do not sit there and beat yourself up. Never gossip.

13. If you're presented with several opportunities at the same time, then sort them into groups: opportunity one, opportunity two, and so forth.

14. Understand that God has unprecedented favor for your life. See it, speak it, and receive it.

15. Put together a solid PLA regarding your opportunity. Without a doubt, there is *no way* I could have made it through countless difficult nights and days without depending totally upon the Word of God.

16. Approach it with a team. Put together a strategic team of big thinkers, which could also include your wise counsel board. Surround yourself with great team members. I would not be where I am today without phenomenal team members. (Note: this is not about a counseling session.)

17. Allow yourself to laugh about that opportunity and laugh at yourself.

18. Stay in shape physically during the opportunity. (See the *15 Healthy Habits* on page 91.)

Keynotes:

- Cornerstones 1–5 represent your life's vehicle.
- Cornerstones 6–11 represent the fuel for that vehicle.
- Rid yourself of *pansy-itis*.
- The road we travel can present many opportunities.
- Problems are opportunities that can catapult you into your greatest hour.
- Stay determined to be strong and courageous! Seize every opportunity with greatness and resolve.
- Run as fast as you can from the temptation to board Pansy-itis Airlines.
- Resolve to board Warrior Airlines.
- Arriving at the promised land will take great resolve and determination.
- The apostle Paul never gave up.
- Use bulldog faith to build up your resolve.
- Shake it off!
- Consider it all joy when you face various trials, rejoicing in the opportunity to build up your faith.
- Use the "Top 18 Ways to Handle Adversity" checklist when you face adversity.
- Don't let adversity define who you are.
- Remain calm and collected in the midst of the storm.
- Ask God for help; ask for His wisdom.

CHAPTER TWENTY-ONE

Cornerstone 8 — Your Accountability

Accountability produces personal responsibility as well as measurable growth. However, pride and fear are often what prevent us from being truly accountable to each other. We need to realize that accountability should work both from the top down and from the bottom up in every family, group, team, business, and organization. Accountability sets expectations in motion on both sides through the use of many types of accountability tools. Even when you go to the bank to borrow money, they use your credit report as an accountability tool.

How does accountability work? Inspect what you expect. Test the integrity. From picking an exercise teacher to picking a financial planner, the options are endless. You can inspect what you expect in every realm of life because accountability engages all parties. Be proactive about developing accountability partners in all areas of your life and establishing daily, weekly, and monthly accountability systems.

Look for accountability partners who will challenge you.

The true test of an effective accountability partner is determining whether someone will challenge and push you. I'm not talking about a drill sergeant screaming insults at you and trying to intimidate you. However, there is no question in my mind that without authentic accountability, you will never reach your true potential. We go further in life *with* other people (the right people) than we do alone. As human beings, we were designed that way. That's why we function best when we work with that "system" innate within each of us.

For accountability to operate at its full potential, you need to develop a system or structure that can measure your growth. One of my favorite examples of someone who does this is Mr.

Alden Smith. This man is not only my friend and mentor, but he's also my personal trainer. I have had a personal trainer for many years, but I have been working with Alden for the last several years. He's a teacher of a healthy lifestyle.

Accountability partners make all the difference.

Don Spear has been a great accountability partner of mine for many years. He is a Christian businessman who walks the talk. In several areas of my life, he has mentored me and held me accountable. At one of the lowest times in my life, Don Spear unequivocally stepped in and took me to a new level of accountability. I'll never forget that.

Then, of course, there was Truett Dodson, the gentleman who started it all. He took the time to share the gospel with me, leading me to the saving knowledge of Jesus Christ. Thank you, Truett.

Look for teammates to hold accountable.

This is where the rubber meets the road because most people don't like to hold others accountable. Sometimes it's easier not to say anything to friends and family, but that's when the real test comes, and when life can really go deep. Not to mention, real men prove to be real men when they hold each other accountable to do the right things. Look for teammates who would like to be held accountable. No doubt, it takes work and discipline, but as you hold other people accountable, it will also help you stay accountable and practice getting better at it.

Accountability sets the tone in the workplace.

True accountability in every position—from ownership to management to entry-level team members—is a developed culture that creates confidence within every team member. Where there is confidence, there is peak performance. It means everyone thinks in terms of ownership. Everyone takes responsibility. Everyone goes to work on themselves, no matter who they are or what position they hold in that organization. It takes work every single day from every team member to maintain this culture of accountability, but it pays off.

On the other hand, without accountability, you find just the opposite within an organization. Everything begins to go downhill. Many companies have gone out of business because people closed their eyes to dishonest business practices and failed to hold upper management accountable. From the least to the greatest, there needs to be accountability. The person in the mailroom is as important as the person in the boardroom. That's what it means to have a culture of accountability.

Simple accountability measures create great leaders.

Accountability is built upon guidelines and rules, with some being much simpler than others. Some accountability systems are laws. Some accountability systems are less official, like guidelines. Accountability systems also vary in function and purpose. Some areas of accountability are put in place to help save lives—either yours or someone else's. Other kinds are meant to better our lives.

Yes, it's tempting to break or bend the rules, but in the long run, you will be better off staying accountable, even with the simplest things. When you start holding yourself accountable to obey the laws, rules, and systems that are put in place, you will be honored by God. The more you stay accountable in the natural, the more you will also be entrusted with the spiritual.

Some of the items listed below are not official laws. However, I am convinced that integrity is all about doing the small things right (even if it's not a law), especially when no one is looking. Here are just a few examples that will set the course of your life in the right direction:

- Drive the speed limit all the time.
- Focus on driving the vehicle without being distracted by other devices.
- Never drive under the influence of drugs or alcohol.
- Always be honest with your taxes.

- Always be honest with an insurance claim.
- Treat other people the way you would want to be treated.
- Never take advantage of someone's lack of experience or education.
- Honor your father and mother.
- Wear your seatbelt.
- Don't partake of illegal drugs.
- Always tell the truth.
- Pay your bills on time.
- Honor your promises.
- Approach all transactions, whether personal or business, with integrity.
- Eradicate vulgar or foul language from your vocabulary.
- Be on time. It's a simple but very important part of accountability.

God's principles are effective accountability tools.

The Bible is God's manual for great accountability. It is not intended to restrict you but just the opposite: to reveal life and to give it to you more abundantly. One of the best accountability lessons of the Bible consists of the Ten Commandments.[75] Notice that it's not the Ten Suggestions. God has so many wonderful promises for you in His Word. The Bible states that "to whom much has been given, much will be required."[76] That's a great principle related to accountability.

Use your Quarterly Personal Assessment for accountability.

In this book are several great tools and checklists to help hold you accountable. One of the most valuable tools is the "Quarterly Personal Assessment." Share this with the people you care about. Have them fill it out for themselves as well. Find the people with whom you can stay accountable to what you both write down. Doing this *will* increase your productivity.

Here are my top ten accountability systems and tools:

1. The scale. Be consistent about checking your weight.
2. Fill out a personal and business financial statement each quarter. (You can get this from your bank.)
3. Ask your spouse three things you can do to improve. Revisit that at least twice a month.
4. Ask your superiors three things you can do to improve. Visit with them at least once a quarter.
5. Exercise a minimum of four times a week.
6. Read a minimum of three hours a week.
7. Ask God what you could do better. Then take time to be quiet with Him, listening to how He answers you.
8. Share the gospel or pray with someone at least one time each month. Be an encouragement.
9. Go one week per month without television.
10. The famous "Mr. Budget" is a very practical means of accountability. Spend less than what comes in. The purpose of a budget is to build wealth.

Keynotes:

- Accountability produces personal responsibility as well as measurable growth.
- Pride and fear often prevent us from staying accountable.
- Practice accountability. Inspect what you expect.
- Develop a system or structure that can measure your growth.
- Look for others whom you can hold accountable and who will hold you accountable to do the right things.
- True accountability creates a culture of confidence from the top down and the bottom up.
- The more you stay accountable in the natural, the more you will also be entrusted with the spiritual.
- Meditate on the power of accountability.

CHAPTER TWENTY-TWO

Cornerstone 9 — The 8 Areas of Your Life

In a lot of circles, you hear people refer to balance as if to say that every area of your life should have the same amount of time and effort put toward it. If that's what balance means, then balance should not be your focus. Your aim is to go to work on *all 8 areas* of your life — none of them are more important than the others. In other words, balance may not mean each area gets the same amount of focus, but none of them should ever be neglected.

There are going to be seasons in your life when you invest more time and dedication into one area, but that does not make it more *important* than the other areas. For example, launching a new business may require more time, energy, and effort than other areas for a time; however, those other areas of your life (like family and rest) should not be totally ignored while you get your business up and running (thus, the importance of planning and systems for each area).

What's the purpose?

We have covered a lot of information about the *8 Areas* of your life. At this time, I would like to give you another perspective, which I believe makes the *8 Areas* important enough to be one of the *11 Cornerstones*.

Having asked many individuals what they believe is the purpose of implementing these *8 Areas*, I've found several most common answers, and they are all true:

1) Using these *8 Areas* adds purpose and meaning to life.

2) It provides you with a foundation and the tools to accomplish more.

3) It adds balance to your life.

The last one is true if the balance is planned properly. But as I said earlier, there are seasons in your life when you may not have balance according to the traditional view of it.

For example, I spoke with someone who was working on getting into medical school, and her roommate told her that she was studying way too much and not enjoying college life. From her roommate's perspective, this was the case. In reality, it was simply a time and season in her life when she had to dedicate a lot of work toward her acceptance into medical school. The same goes for anyone in training to become a Navy SEAL. I think you get the point.

Balance may mean more time in one area as long as the other areas are still appropriately supported and functioning at the same time. No area gets left out. Again, strategic planning will be key.

Now, what is the point of saying all this? What is the real purpose of being aware of and implementing the *8 Areas* of your life? Mentioned previously (in Spiritual Alignment #10), the purpose is for you to be a bright, bright light to the world around you, which is a fruit of you living a fulfilling life, which is the result of thriving in all *8 Areas* of your life.

I would rather watch a winner than hear one any day.

When it comes down to it, your actions always speak louder — big-time louder — than your words. As we also covered earlier, you may have real success in one or two areas of your life, but the other areas end up lacking or missing. That's where the benefit of implementing the *8 Areas* comes into play. How will you know how to successfully manage every area of your life if you're not even aware of them? On the other hand, planning for them is like creating architectural plans and blueprints of how to build a life of excellence, one which everyone else would be able to recognize.

People naturally gravitate to light. Even when we look at photographs, the first thing our eyes naturally gravitate toward is the brightest spot in the photo. We also naturally imitate whatever we value. Now, let's put those characteristics together.

When others see the light of us winning big in life, we position ourselves to reproduce that light because others will want to walk in the same light. When others see our light and value it, then that light begins to reproduce itself in them. This is how a legacy is made, and it's a part of your high calling to leave a legacy! It's also easier than you'd think.

Fasten your seatbelts: this may sound strong.

In many sectors of Christianity, it's all too common for people not to "walk the talk." They use a lot of spiritual words, but their integrity may be questionable. They may have a good heart, but their actions are inconsistent with their values. They don't take care of their bodies, and their lives are a mess.

In one group, the majority of those people often have poor or bad credit, and they don't recognize the inconsistency of their testimony. They certainly talk a big game, but their actions don't line up with what they say. I was one of them for many years. I bounced checks even to Christian organizations. It was pathetic and embarrassing.

Please understand: I'm not condemning anyone, nor do I suggest it. I'm talking about recognizing that even though these kinds of people love God, their actions behind the scenes are inconsistent with what they're saying. I know that sounds tough, but I've noticed it enough that it needs to be said. Why? It's critical that we recognize and turn from hypocrisy in every area of our lives. Every double standard is an open door to greater inconsistency. Here's the point: I lived a life just like that, and God turned it around as He gave me His wisdom in doing the small things right in every area of my life. It's not that I've arrived at the point of never making mistakes or poor choices; I know I'm not perfect. I'm still in a process, but I am consistently and intentionally practicing to better myself in every area.

Set the record straight in all *8 Areas*.

Once you recognize the double standard in your life, acknowledge it before God, asking Him to forgive you, and then *set the record straight*. Go to the people or institutions to whom you owe money and to those whom you misled. Believe it or not, this is exactly what I did. If I owed someone money, I went to them and paid the money back with interest (except for my mother, because she was already in heaven). I asked God to forgive me for being such a flake. And guess what? He forgave me! By the way, the people I misled also forgave me. Wow! God is so good.

I mentioned in the first chapter of this book that your commitment has power. Your commitment to walk with integrity in every area of your life has power. As you walk in this integrity, with a testimony that is consistent with your words, your life will shine as a bright light to everyone around you and you will even enjoy your own life more. What are you waiting for? Today is *the big day* to go for it!

Keynotes:

- Your aim is to work on *all 8 Areas* of your life—none of them are more important than the others.
- There are going to be seasons in your life when you invest more time and dedication into one area, but that does not make it more *important* than the other areas.
- Strategic planning will be key.
- Planning for all *8 Areas* is like creating architectural plans and blueprints of how to build a life of excellence.
- It's a part of your high calling to leave a legacy.
- Being a bright light for others will inevitably be reproduced in them. This is how a legacy is made.
- Recognize any double standards in your life and set the record straight.
- Practice walking with integrity in all *8 Areas* of your life.

CHAPTER TWENTY-THREE

Cornerstone 10 — Your Work Ethic

Work implies action, and ethic refers to values. Action plus values equals work ethic. Whether you have clearly defined them, you hold a set of values, and it can take work to live according to the values you know you hold. It takes effort and action to maintain those values and grow in them yourself. Thus, you have a certain work ethic.

Work ethic changes you from the inside out.

Where does work ethic begin? On the inside of you. First, work on yourself regarding your mind, will, and emotions. You should not take a day off from that inner project. Next, focus on each of the *8 Areas* of your life one at a time.

For example, you should work on your wealth plan. But how many people actually do that? I'm not talking about your job. I literally mean your wealth plan, like planning and pursuing multiple streams of income.

What about your work ethic regarding your health plan? Sweating and exercise are good, but it takes hard work to reach greater goals in your health. It even takes work to rest according to your rest plan. You'll need to be quiet and silent for a change and turn off all the electronic devices and media, including television, to legitimately quiet your brain. At first, when you pull away from those electronic caffeine mechanisms, it will be tough, and that's why it's going to take work. Changing habits requires work ethic. You can have a plan and a strategy for each of the *8 Areas* of your life, but intentionally living out those goals requires the right work ethic.

So, it's going to take work. Let me say it a little differently. It's going to take a great, great work ethic, along with discipline and pain, to achieve a level of excellence in each of the *8 Areas* of your life. Nothing great has ever been accomplished by being soft, lackadaisical, loosey-goosey, half-hearted, or, the granddaddy—someday getting lucky. That's why the devil loves the words *easy, lucky,* and *snooze button.* He loves when we say, "Don't work so hard. Don't get up early. Don't be an overachiever. You don't have time to exercise or read your Bible." Giving in to these thoughts threatens your work ethic and potential of winning big.

Is your work ethic headed in the wrong direction?

We often sell ourselves so short when we agree with mind-sets (or values) such as, "I've put in my forty hours. I'm not doing anything else this week. I'll just make it to retirement and then do nothing but play golf and sleep in. I'll be fine living only on my retirement income. Average is OK. I don't need to try so hard. I don't have time to exercise. I'm too old. Weekends are not for being productive. Going into business for myself is too risky, and odds are I'll fail." All of those may be half-truths at best, but the reality is that these kinds of thoughts are the training ground that the enemy uses to get our mind-set about work ethic headed in the wrong direction. Why? To thwart our effectiveness.

You were designed in "God-class."

Designed in the image of our Creator (God),[77] we are hardwired for great accomplishment. We are called and fashioned to be a light in our work and our values. God loves work ethic because it expresses His image in us and in who we are. The more we express His image, the more we shine as a light.

The Bible is plain in declaring that we are heirs of God through Jesus.[78] It also pronounces us priests and kings.[79] Those three facts alone place us in a position of authority. We understand that it is not by our strength or our might.

However, simply stated many times throughout the Bible, it's the authenticity of God's grace and the blood of Jesus that gives us this authority. As believers, God lives within our hearts,[80] and it's our mind that needs to be renewed in order to understand the authority that we have in Him. The renewing of our mind gives us a quiet confidence and a bold inner witness that we are truly covenant partners with God. That is powerful.

Once you begin to comprehend that you are truly made in "God-class," designed for great works with the authority of God behind you, then watch what happens! Emotional highs and lows will disappear, and your life will be steady, consistent with the art of practicing discipline in all *8 Areas* of your life.

Remember how the natural and spiritual forces operate together? Our work ethic is a natural application of a spiritual reality, and the purpose and meaning of our lives are also expressed through our work ethic. We are top-of-the-line when it comes to how we're made. That's good news! What we do with who we are is our choice. And that's a daily walk, each and every *big day*.

What's your mind-set about work ethic?

I've noticed that most unsuccessful people blame the economy and various controllable circumstances for their difficult situations. Truth be told, many of them play instead of work while they're "on the clock," or, as I call it, they "play-work." Sales is one of the most famous vocations for masking work. I have no doubt that a high percentage of salespeople are play-working, also described as performing busywork. (Not everyone though, of course.)

Contrary to this, I had a very successful businessman give me some of the best advice I've ever heard. He told me to work half-days. He said he didn't care which half. Now, that doesn't mean half of a regular eight-hour workday; it means half of a regular twenty-four-hour day. Talk about a paradigm shift in work ethic!

Hectic weekends have become the norm.

Around the world today, culture has produced weekends that will never be the same again. That's not necessarily a bad thing.

Nowadays, hundreds of thousands of people work on weekends. Perhaps that's due to a second job, or perhaps your job is in one of the industries among many that work weekends, like retail, hospitality, medical, sports, communication, real estate, public service, or the military. We could go on and on with hundreds of different industries. The point is, many of us lead very busy lives going in thousands of different directions, and the pace of our lives continues to accelerate. Life is constantly moving faster and faster, becoming more complicated as we speak.

Work ethic changes the status quo of weekends.

Does your work ethic change when the weekend comes around? We weren't meant to separate the weekday from the weekend, as if they were two totally different parts of our lives. On the contrary, every day of every week is meant for us to grow in all *8 Areas* of our lives. That includes weekends!

But oftentimes we take a break from our real lives and/or working on ourselves, and we end up losing the power of *the big day* on the weekend. I propose that we retrain our thinking about the weekend! Let's take a closer look at this.

How's your weekend shaping up?

Perhaps an even better question would be: *Who* is shaping up your weekend? Despite the busyness of our lives, we are constantly being trained by the so-called mainstream views of the world on what our weekends should look like, sometimes to our detriment. Here are some examples:

- TGIF—no more work! Finally, the weekend is here and you are off from everything!
- Eat excessively, drink excessively, and celebrate the weekend!
- It's time for your golf game for the weekend, and, of course, a few drinks along the way.
- It's Friday (or Saturday) night. Go to a restaurant! Everyone knows that's what you're supposed to do.

- It's the weekend! Throw caution to the wind. You don't have any responsibilities and absolutely no need for discipline!
- Go to church; you need to save your conscience.
- Don't forget the home shows, the boat shows, the RV shows, the gun shows, and the car shows. After all, it only takes 5 to 10 percent down and you can own a brand-new _____. You're not really living if you don't know about the newest and best of all that's out there! In fact, you really need it for yourself too.
- Saturday and Sunday — the big retail days! Get it before it's gone! Don't miss the sales! Make sure you make it out to the malls, and don't worry about food. The malls always have healthy and delicious options at the food courts.
- Family time: first little league, then soccer, then errands, then _____. It's OK to rush from one event to another every weekend, as long as you're together!
- Read the *New York Times* in bed. It's relaxing: Who got shot? Who got killed? The chaos. The confusion. Fill your head with all the "good news" before you start your day — especially on Sunday, when the paper is even thicker with good news!
- Don't leave out the Sunday morning news and talk shows. You need to know what everyone is talking about! Wow, what would you do without all that positive information? (Again, this is how we're being trained!)
- Adult recess: go to the bars! Drink as much as you want. Ride mechanical bulls and dance the night away like they do in the movies.
- Weekends were made for great parties and excessive drinking. It's like spring break every weekend! If it's not like that, you're missing out!
- Hollywood got it right: Like cowboys in western shows, you're supposed to go into town on Saturday night for (of course) the drinking, gambling, and fighting. The

weekend is even better if someone gets shot or goes to jail. (All this is in good humor in the movies, but we receive it as our reality.)

- Friday and Saturday nights—let the mayhem begin! Never mind the zoo of people on drugs and alcohol. It's OK. It's normal.
- Don't miss any big games and matches (of sports from A to Z). Keep up with all the players too! Friday, Saturday, and Sunday—all weekend long, nonstop action!
- It's time for tailgating! If you're going to any major college or pro football event, then get the drinks out! It's no fun without food that's over the top and drinks that make you feel good! (Obviously, that doesn't mean lemonade or soda pop.)
- Finally, the granddaddy of them all: the classic hangover! Wow, wasn't that fun, not to mention everything else that goes along with it. What a great weekend.

I'm not discounting or making fun of any of the above. Personally, I'm no stranger to most of them. However, I would like to give you a different perspective for retraining and developing yourself in order to have a big-time *successful* weekend.

Sadly, the perspective of some people goes something like this: "I've worked for five days at the salt mines. I get two days off for my good behavior all week." In other words, what they're saying is, "I've been diligently doing the right things for five days, and now I'm going to go off and do things that could be potentially unproductive or detrimental to my life."

Engaging in unproductive or detrimental activities gets you distracted all too easily. You could (and often will) lose the ground and momentum that you worked so hard for during those five days because you feel like you "deserve" to let go—just because it's the weekend! I know what it's like to lose joy in all *8 Areas* of my life simply because I lost the importance of those two days. I'm not just talking about partying and going crazy. I'm talking about behavior that sets you back and causes you to lose focus.

Moreover, could it be that people commonly suffer from the so-called "Monday Blues" because they don't feel they can have fun, fulfillment, and freedom during the week like they can on the weekend? Thus, they always end up dreading the week ahead. I am convinced this is a consequence of the paradigm that separates weekdays from weekends.

Work ethic and rest actually work together.

Weekends are no different than any other days of the week when it comes to your rest plan. Just as it is for all other areas of your life, rest is still for *every day* of the week, even though you may dedicate more time to your rest plan one or two days a week (depending on what your weekends are like).

How do we retrain our thinking about weekends?

One of my mentors said weekends should be called "week-ups," not weekends. Renaming them retrains your thinking and mind-set. In other words, we're going to end strong. The weekend should be a great and fulfilling time.

There are many ways to retrain your paradigm about weekends. The items below are just a few creative examples of what your weekends can look like when your mind-set is transformed. Some of the items (if not all of them) will take work, practice, and planning. Just start small. Remember to plan but don't over-plan. When it comes to retraining your thinking about weekends, one of the biggest points to remember is to change your routine.

Win big on your week-ups.

The items below can be done with your family, friends, spouse, by yourself, etc.

- Establish a work ethic in all *8 Areas* of your life.
- Have a simple plan, not jam-packed.

- Don't overextend your weekends with your to-do list. You're not in a weekend race!
- Train yourself to be quiet and turn off all distractions, especially all electronic devices, in order to develop a quiet mind-set. Retrain your paradigm of what rest and relaxation look like.
- Limit excessive eating; instead, eat extremely healthy food and quantities. (Having said that, I like to eat a somewhat unhealthy meal once a weekend or so, just not in excess.)
- Abstain from alcohol, TV, and (if you're like me, this is going to be tough) sports all weekend.
- Take a walk of at least one to five miles.
- Make time to think intentionally.
- Do something totally different or out of the ordinary.
- Build a vision board for all *8 Areas* of your life. This includes pictures that reflect what you envision in every area. Cut or print them out and post them where you can see them every day. Whatever it is you want—like a more peaceful life, more sales for your business, or better health—a vision board adds the color to your vision.
- Keep a gratitude journal. This is so, so important.
- Do one thing per weekend that will produce excellence in your life.
- If you have a Monday-through-Friday desk job, then do something physical on the weekends, like plant a small garden, wash your car by hand, or even do simple exercises. Some people's idea of physical exercise is filling up the bathtub, getting in it, unplugging the drain, and fighting the current. (That's a joke.)
- Practice releasing everything—every single care, every single anxious thought and feeling—to our God. I practice this for at least thirty minutes on Saturday or Sunday. It's like being on vacation for a week.
- Do something nice for your neighbor or friend.
- Volunteer for a great cause. But it's very, very important not to volunteer in excess.

- Write a letter at least once a month to somebody you admire and mail it to them. The fun part is trying to get their address.
- Meet one new person each month, especially in your neighborhood.
- Have some romantic time with your spouse. Make it fun.
- Crash someone's wedding! Just kidding.
- Prepare for your upcoming week.
- Work on your wealth plan.
- At least once a weekend, have adult playtime without alcohol or sports.
- Declutter your life. Practice the art of saying, "No, thank you."
- Practice smiling throughout the weekend.
- I've said it before, but I'm going say it again: limit your alcohol intake, or avoid it altogether. It really does not help you relax—just the opposite. We do not need alcohol to have fun, but we've been trained to believe that we do. For example, there was a time when I thought it was impossible to have a great tailgate without alcohol. But it's just not the case! I really enjoy the game so much more being 100 percent sober.
- Take time to rearrange and reshape your priorities and what's important to you.
- Decide that, from Friday at 5 p.m. to Monday at 5 a.m., you will not complain or say any ugly words, especially to your loved ones. Wear a rubber band around your wrist, and every time you do complain or say something ugly, pop yourself.
- Drive a different way to your destination and/or drive a different way home. This stimulates creativity.
- Take a minimum of fifteen minutes each weekend to praise God for what He's done in your life.
- Over the span of a year, some of my favorite things to do on weekends include: visiting the botanical garden, visiting different types of museums, spending some time at the library, going to a park, going to a musical, riding

a bicycle, helping with a prison ministry, attending a cooking school, riding my motorcycle, doing creative writing, being a tourist in my own city, trying out a new restaurant, cooking something from scratch that I've never made before, sending at least two encouraging texts to someone, visiting the zoo, taking a nap, getting a full-body massage, and deep breathing and stretching.

The items listed above are just a few examples. The important thing is to come up with creative ideas yourself to consistently change what you are doing on weekends in order to make them week-ups whether your weekend is Saturday and Sunday, Monday or Tuesday, one day a week or two, etc. Once you start these procedures and systems, you will see your mental acuity actually start to develop for the best. You will see rising levels of productivity in all *8 Areas* of your life, all seven days of the week.

This may sound over the top, but you will also begin to see God like you've never seen Him before. Your relationships with God and people will start soaring to new heights.

Just by practicing the above, disciplining yourself to change your routine on the weekend (especially for six months or more), I guarantee that your life will turn a revolutionary corner and improve in both the natural and the spiritual.

Work ethic doesn't end after work.

Work ethic can obviously consist of mental capacities as well as physical. Let me give you some practical examples of different types of work ethics. Maybe you have accomplished some of these, or maybe you've never thought of them. Some might be necessary for you right now. Also, some will probably be harder than others to implement. The point is to develop your work ethic to its greatest potential for evenings or weekends, or anytime you're away from school, work, your career, or your company.

- Intentionally and strategically plan for a productive and restful evening or week-up.
- For some, it may take hard work and discipline to train yourself to unplug from everything. This especially includes your phone, computer, and television.
- Look at your finances and analyze what may need to change or be done. Review your investments and study others.
- Have meaningful conversations with your team members and find out their needs.
- Slow your pace.
- Give yourself absolute silence and do nothing for an extended period. Start with thirty minutes, then work your way up. (This one takes a lot of work for most people.)
- Take some time to reflect on your priorities, potentially eliminating some of the things you're doing now. Another way to say this is, stop the roller coaster of your life. Get off and examine why you're even on the roller coaster in the first place.
- Organize and remove some, or all, of the clutter in areas such as your car, pantry, kitchen, closets, garage, and filing system. You'll feel a lot better and clear-minded.
- Plan and organize certain events, like your vacations. It can be as simple as being a tourist in your own city or one nearby. Come up with strategies for events in different areas of your life.
- My all-time favorite work ethic is setting thirty minutes to an hour just to talk with God; this is life-transforming.
- Decide to be diligent in examining all *8 Areas* of your life. (The "Quarterly Personal Assessment" on page 146 is a great tool you can use to help you see where you are, so that you know where you're going. Fill it out once a quarter.)

We could cover a thousand more examples of work ethics, but hopefully this gives you some ideas for your own life, or at least a place for you to start developing your work ethics today. It's a wise and prudent way to grow in every area of your life. The Bible offers insight to this very topic when it says, "The plans of the diligent lead surely to plenty."[81] That sums it up right there.

Use your time wisely.

I would like to add another important note. You may be in a season of your life when you don't have a lot of time off or time for other activities. No matter how much time you *do* have, whether it's one half-day a month or two days a quarter, use that time wisely. Don't lose focus, but have a plan for how to make it as productive as possible, even if that means planning your rest.

Add work ethic to all that you're practicing.

We've discussed the word *practice* in detail in previous chapters. Hopefully, you've already been able to apply it to your own situations. Practice also relates to work ethic. Both rest *and* work are fulfilling when you're practicing the wisdom of God, being led by His Spirit, and developing your faith. When you then add a determined work ethic to the mix, prepare yourself for a life that's above and beyond!

Consistency is for every day.

To stay consistent with our checklists, I would like to give you what I consider some of the toughest areas to begin working on, let alone to *continue* working on every day. (It's going to take work ethic!) As you already know, work can be physical or mental or both. In fact, I believe mental work can sometimes be more taxing than physical work. Thus, it takes the mentality of a warrior to consistently work on the toughest areas. See the next page for your warrior checklist.

WARRIOR CHECKLIST

✓ Cast down any thought that opposes what God's Word says about your life or your team members' lives.

✓ Speak words of faith. Call forth those things that are not (yet) as though they were. (e.g., "I have the greatest work ethic of anyone I know.")

✓ Speak words that are always full of life. Refuse to let any words come out of your mouth that contradict your potential.

✓ Choose to put the right things in your mouth.

✓ Discipline your emotions — not letting your emotions rule over you, but taking authority over how your emotions affect you.

✓ Remain unoffendable. Discipline yourself never to be offended.

✓ Exercise a minimum of four times a week.

✓ Have a believing heart. Continue in faith even when it doesn't look like it's working. Never, ever, ever give up on this.

Work ethic is key to achieving our dream goals as well as excellence in values. Work ethic is everyday fuel for your vehicle in life.

Keynotes:

- Work plus values equals work ethic.
- We express the purpose and meaning of our lives through our work ethic.
- You are destined for great accomplishment because you're made in "God-class."
- Our work is a natural application of a spiritual reality.
- Work ethic begins on the inside of you and works its way out to the *8 Areas* of your life.
- Changing habits requires work ethic.
- Retrain your paradigm of weekends.
- Don't lose focus on the weekend. Use all free time wisely.
- Include rest in your work ethic.
- Work ethic is everyday fuel for your vehicle in life.

CHAPTER TWENTY-FOUR

Cornerstone 11 — Thankfulness

Thankfulness is the door that opens your world up to a whole new level of possibilities! When you practice thankfulness, your focus shifts from what is not working to what is working. It is truly hard to be grumpy and complain while being thankful at the same time. Choosing to be thankful creates a spirit of gratitude that stays with you all the time. It is your choice, but believe me, *thankfulness is fuel that allows your life to go further than it ever would have without it*. It uncaps your potential of winning big and immediately catapults you into greatness.

Being thankful will help you through the tough times. It will help you refocus and understand what both you and God have already accomplished. Being thankful also takes the focus off all the distractions in life. It produces both the posture of humility and the perspective of a warrior.

Be aware that it does take work (especially at the beginning) to form this as a habit. I recommend that you start by making a list of what you're thankful for, which could include events, places, people, and even God. Not only that, but God's promises are always there for you. They are working on your behalf even when you're not aware of it. That's always something to be thankful for!

Short and sweet: we are blessed!

Americans are truly blessed. Most of the world's population today does not have the everyday amenities that we often take for granted. A very successful businessman from Africa once said to me that living in America is like living in a candy store. I can absolutely see why he says that.

Thankfulness produces courteous and polite behavior.

Thankfulness is a common fruit in the lives of people who are characteristically polite and courteous. Have you ever noticed that? Something that we all need to practice each day is treating people in an honorable way, especially the ones who serve you in a very courteous manner. Take notice of them. Practice looking them in the eye and using the words *please* and *thank you* over and over. Start adding these words to your vocabulary throughout the day, like seasoning on your food.

In the past, when I worked with customers, I know that if a customer had been over-the-top rude, even though they may have had a right to be rude, typically they would get far less from me in the long run. But, if they were courteous, I would do almost anything. That's just human nature.

But now, I practice making the quality decision to go above and beyond that. I encourage you to do the same, being courteous, kind, and lovely, even to the uncourteous, unkind and unlovely. I know you may be thinking, "Well, they don't deserve it, and, besides, if I do that, they could take advantage of me or the situation." Maybe so, but regardless of that, I've decided to go out of my way to be courteous and polite to everyone with whom I interact, *especially when I don't feel like it*. Not only will this cultivate thankfulness in me, but it will also plant seeds of thankfulness in others as well.

We all have bad hair days, and that's OK.

Give people a chance to have a bad hair day (especially your wife — just kidding). Obviously, I'm not talking about abuse. I'm simply saying, train yourself to bite your tongue. I believe that's one of the main reasons God gave us our teeth (also kidding).

In other words, don't say everything you may be thinking when someone doesn't measure up to your standards. When you're graceful, loving, and kind, you are sowing seeds that will come back to you in even greater measure. Giving people the benefit of the doubt and putting a big smile on your face are seeds of power (again, especially when you don't feel like it). This is one of the top things I've continually worked on because I am a perfectionist and expect people to give as much as I'm giving. That's just an unrealistic expectation on my part.

If someone makes a comment with which you don't agree, you don't have to give everyone your opinion about it. Besides, they might actually be right, but even if they aren't, don't make a federal case out of it. Regardless of your disagreement, speak life over them. Why? It opens channels of blessings over that person *and* over your life. Practice opening yourself up to a spirit of thankfulness and graciousness.

Thankfulness is one of the main characteristics of love.

I love the part in the Bible which describes how you can appear to be the greatest Christian in the world, yet if you don't have love, then you are only like a clanging gong, making a lot of useless noise.[82] Anytime you are rude or discourteous to anyone, it's fruit that is contrary to the Spirit of God and doesn't display love.

On the flip side of that coin, when you have love, then the fruit of thankfulness and graciousness, and, most importantly, forgiveness, will truly speak volumes to people, and they will actually be drawn to it. Here's the most amazing part: when you're thankful, you will feel one hundred pounds lighter, like you're no longer carrying the weight of the world.

(Note: Thankfulness does not question or accuse God concerning your situation. Doing that never make sense! It's like trying to separate the natural and the spiritual.) All this is to say, go out of your way to be thankful. Practice being thankful for the small things every single day. Wow!

I could write a series on the Chronicles of Thankfulness.

What am I thankful for? Well, the list runs so long that I could easily make it into a book. I could even write a subsequent book filled with just the names of all the people for whom I am extremely thankful. Most importantly, that would include my wife, Nancy. I believe I would not be where I am without her, as well as the other people I have in mind. Beyond all that, there is absolutely no way that I would be alive, much less have the mental faculties that allowed me to be where I am today, without God's grace and without all that Jesus did for me on Calvary. That could be another book on its own.

Here's the top twelve on my Thankful List:

- My God
- The Bible
- The day I gave my life to Christ
- My wife, Nancy (the love of my life)
- My family
- Truett Dodson
- Don Spear
- My business teams and vendors (past, present, and future), along with their families
- My church (my spiritual team)
- My mentors (all one-hundred-plus of them)
- Many inspiring books, YouTube videos, and seminars
- Jill Blue, Heather Lester, Yvonne Avila, and Alden Smith

I'm also extremely thankful for everyone reading this book. My encouragement to you is to read it several times and put the content into practice in your own life, starting today. Why wait any longer?

Today is not just any day. Today is your *big day*.

Go for it!

Keynotes:

- Thankfulness creates possibilities.
- Thankfulness shifts your focus from what is not working to what is working.
- Being thankful will help you through the tough times.
- It produces both the posture of humility and the perspective of a warrior.
- God's promises are working on your behalf whether you're aware of it.
- Thankfulness is fuel for *the big day*.

Did you like what you've read?

I sincerely hope you enjoyed reading this book as much as I enjoyed writing it. If you did, I would greatly appreciate a short review on Amazon or your favorite book website. Reviews are crucial for any author, and even just a line or two can make a huge difference.

Scan the QR code for instant access to my Amazon author page, or visit this link: www.amazon.com/author/whipple

Who is Robert W. Whipple?

Coach. Business Owner. Public Speaker. Author. TCU Fan. Life Enthusiast.

Robert Whipple is both the Vice President of Operations and Training and the owner of multiple franchises for one of the largest home improvement companies in Texas. He is involved in many nonprofit ventures, and he is currently on the Board of Directors of the Texas Christian University Fellowship of Christian Athletes. Robert and his wife, Nancy, currently reside in Fort Worth, Texas, and have been happily married for over forty years.

Robert Whipple also has more than thirty years of experience in leading and coaching numerous teams and individuals in business as well as life. As a public speaker, Robert has addressed groups such as civic organizations, city chambers, business clubs, and churches. He is well-known for his likability, his "never-been-better" attitude, his openness to new concepts and ideas from team members, and the way he constantly works to improve himself and encourages others to do the same. One of his favorite pastimes is riding his motorcycle.

As founder of The Big Day®, his passion is to create a culture of leaders who are successful physically, mentally, emotionally, and spiritually. He possesses both the motivation and the expertise to see others win big in every area of their lives.

Connect with The Big Day® Team

The Big Day® is a virtual life coach and resource platform designed to establish a culture of successful leaders. From podcasts and video archives to blog posts and beyond, our vision is to provide you with tools that help you live *all 8 Areas* of your life to the fullest. Check out our website today for the latest updates and the newest resources available!

Visit us now at www.readyforthebigday.com, or scan the QR code below:

You can also email us (info@readyforthebigday.com) and find us on Facebook, Twitter, Instagram, Pinterest, SoundCloud, and more!

Request a Speaking Engagement with Robert Whipple

If you like what you've read, you'll love it in person! Invite Robert Whipple to speak to your team, service club, company, church, or at your next event.

He is ready to share more about any of the content covered in this book, and additional topics include:

- Getting More Done in Less Time
- Discovering a Better You
- How to Raise Your Income Annually
- Time Management Skillsets
- The Science of Building a Great Business
- Don't Quit Your Day Job

Topics can be covered in a time frame that suits your schedule. For more details, contact us at info@readyforthebigday.com or by visiting our website at www.readyforthebigday.com/contact.

Here are the checklists found throughout the book, which have been divided according to chapters. The tables and forms from the book can be found in *Appendix II*.

CHAPTER THREE

The 8 Areas of your life

1. Spiritual
2. School/Job/Career
3. Health
4. Financial
5. Hobbies
6. Rest
7. Powerful Learning Agenda (PLA)
8. Family/Friends

Several methods I have used not to succumb to defeat during the storms

- Draw near to God through the Scriptures. Meditate upon them throughout the day and into the night. (Here's a note on retraining your thinking: if you can't sleep, that is the best time to read your Bible or at least pray.)
- Get professional, godly counseling.
- Don't try to connect all the dots or answer all the unanswered questions in your own reasoning.
- Surround yourself with team members who are praying for you and encouraging you. I am so thankful for my team members.
- Stay focused on being grateful for the thousands of blessings, literally, that God has brought into your life. Remind yourself of these blessings over and over throughout the day.
- Stay plugged in by serving people, serving your team, and getting your mind off yourself.

- Get up, get dressed, clean yourself up, wash your face, fix your hair, put on your best clothes, and top it off with your favorite cologne. (Women: put your makeup on as well, and wear your favorite perfume.)
- Take one day at a time.
- Go to the gym, go for a jog, or take a long walk outside.
- Speak words of life over yourself, your team, and your family.
- Decide to never ever, ever take your family or teammates for granted.

CHAPTER FOUR

Wisdom Checklist

- Every day, throughout the day, practice walking in the wisdom of God and being led by the Spirit of God.
- Study and meditate on the Word of God several times a day.
- Be calm and peaceful in your day-to-day activities.
- Be extremely disciplined spiritually, mentally, and physically, and always improve in these with a ferocious Powerful Learning Agenda (PLA).
- Practice developing your faith daily.
- Have a great exercise regimen, including two cardio and two core exercises per week.
- Never move forward with a decision based only on how good something looks.
- Don't focus on or be consumed by things over which you have no control, especially people.
- Follow effective time-management principles with a plan for all *8 Areas* of your life.
- Have great systems and written goals for all *8 Areas* of your life.

- Practice implementing wisdom in your speech; be careful about what you say.
- See yourself as a wise person making wise and prudent choices.
- Sow a minimum of 10 percent of your finances into great works.
- Understand that the beginning is the most important part of any endeavor. Spend the amount of time that is necessary for proper preparation.
- Focus on today with an understanding of the future.
- Align yourself with great people and groups.
- When you face a problem, call it an opportunity and handle it with calmness and peace.
- Instead of being easily offended, upset, or lashing out at people, be patient and open to understanding others.
- Be a kind individual to all people.
- Be careful of what you consume in your body.
- Never base decisions on following the crowd.
- Be grateful for what you've been given.
- Don't try to figure everything out in your own strength.
- Challenge your team and other people to be their best.
- Ensure your level of integrity is second to none.
- Always take the initiative.
- Have a great work ethic for all *8 Areas* of your life.
- Be accountable and hold your team accountable.
- Understand that money is simply a tool.
- See the best in people; refuse to be critical.
- Be a skilled, top producer in all that you do. Be way above average.

CHAPTER SEVEN

Wisdom's Checklist of the Past

- The date you committed or recommitted your life to Christ
- Days and "marker moments" when you decided to make a positive change to improve your life
- Special holidays or events with loved ones
- Taking the bad decisions that you made and turning that negative situation into a great opportunity to catapult you to greatness
- Past movies and television shows that are classics.
- Special pictures of events and loved ones
- Learning how to keep from making the same mistake over and over
- Having a track record of taking care of your health
- Being able to laugh at yourself with all the funny things you've done, e.g., disco dancing, wearing leisure suits, or owning shag carpet
- Believing that anything is possible with God
- Honoring the sacrifice of people who lay down their lives for our freedom; this includes policemen, firefighters, the military, etc.
- Great events that have shaped America or the world
- Great revivals and spiritual awakenings in the past
- Not allowing yourself to get caught up in the drama of others and their pasts
- Making the choice (as often as necessary) to agree with words of life over yourself instead of engaging in negative self-talk
- Refusing to dwell on the past
- Reading great books and biographies written by coaches, leaders, revivalists, etc. whose lives were touched by God and who influenced many others
- Spending time studying and meditating on the Holy Bible, inspired by the words of God, teaching all

human beings how to live great (abundant) lives today

CHAPTER EIGHT

Your checklist for the future

- Create short-term goals: zero to twelve months from today.
- Create long-term goals: twelve months to five years from today.
- Schedule events and appointments that promote each of the *8 Areas*. This goes for short-, medium-, and long-term goals.
- Create and maintain a life to-do list, otherwise known as an Expect Great Things (EGT) list.
- Invest into the future with your time and resources today.
- Plan strategic systems for new businesses and the growth of existing businesses.
- Establish strategic plans that develop partnerships with new team members. (Note: team members include our family members, business partners or co-workers, and friends.)
- Build partnerships to set up multiple streams of income. This is to get money working for you so that you're not working for money.
- Implement strategic plans that cultivate growth and coaching for existing team members.
- Create a list of "The Top 50 People I Want to Meet."
- Produce vision boards for each of the *8 Areas* of your life.

CHAPTER TEN

The "Big Guns" Checklist

- This is going to be my greatest hour.
- Greater is He that is in me, than he that is in the problem.

- I am blessed coming in and I'm blessed going out.
- The Lord is my Helper, and I will not fear.
- I will set my thoughts on "whatever is true . . . whatever is pure . . . whatever is lovely."
- "Beloved, I pray that you may prosper in all things and be in health, just as your soul prospers."
- No weapon formed against me will prosper.
- The Lord is my Shepherd, and I shall not want.
- God has not given me a spirit of fear, but of love, power, and a sound mind.
- My God shall supply all my needs according to His riches in glory by Christ Jesus.
- I cast all my cares upon my Lord for He cares for me.
- Be strong and of good courage! Fear not!
- Whoever is born of God overcomes the world and this is the victory that overcomes the world — my faith.
- For I am persuaded that neither death, nor life, nor angels, nor principalities, nor powers, nor things present, nor things to come, nor height, nor depth, nor any other created thing shall be able to separate me from the love of God.

The ingredients of a bad decision.

- Feeling an urgency to "make a decision right now"
- Being sloppy or disorganized
- Being loosey-goosey (careless, noncommittal)
- Being extremely emotionally charged
- Being emotionally disassociated
- Feeling freaked out
- Feeling nervous or overanxious (a bundle of nerves)
- Being fearful about the outcome
- Having to meet a deadline
- Receiving devastating news
- Hyperventilating
- Feeling "scared out of your mind"

- Being emotionally distraught
- Walking in strife with others
- Being upset
- Reading or listening to the news
- Starting to play the what-if game
- Questioning God
- Being upset with your spouse or friend
- Following the crowd
- Expecting the worst
- Overindulging in junk food
- Overindulging in alcohol
- Consuming illegal drugs or overly consuming prescription drugs that alter your thinking
- Feeling pressured by a friend or loved one
- Feeling intimidated
- Being lazy or lacking discipline
- Being extremely agitated
- Feeling exhausted
- Being money-motivated
- Having a mind-set that it's "greener on the other side"
- Feeling that it's a once-in-a-lifetime opportunity
- Living from the negative experiences of your past
- Living in fear of the future
- Rushing past the beginning

The ingredients of a wise decision.

- Consistently walking in *God's* wisdom
- Being led by the Spirit of God
- Having wise counsel — this is big!
- Using the "4-to-1 Rule"
- Lining your actions up with the Word of God
- Spending sufficient time in the beginning of an endeavor
- Being uncomfortable but not fearful
- Developing a plan for each type of decision

- Training yourself to be emotionally stable in the decision-making process
- Being able to laugh at yourself
- Being willing to stretch your current belief system so that you can rise to a new level
- Not overly focusing on the past or the future
- Sensing the peace of God
- Stretching your faith
- Having a Powerful Learning Agenda (PLA)
- Practicing discipline and self-control
- Having an articulated plan and written goals
- Being willing to do something you've never done, which is beneficial to you and/or others
- Not trying to be perfect
- Intending to practice getting better in that endeavor
- Visualizing the outcome
- Doing what most people would consider strange
- Being organized and neat
- Walking in the fruit of the Spirit of God

CHAPTER ELEVEN

The 5 Most Important Questions

1. What are you expecting today?
2. How do you see yourself today?
3. What are you doing today to improve yourself?
4. What words are you speaking today to frame your future?
5. Are you treating this as the most important day of your life?

15 Healthy Habits

1. Get A-Z examinations: physical, dental, skin, etc. This puts you ahead of the curve and on the offense when it comes to your health. (Note: if you don't like your doctors, find ones you do like.)
2. Drink a lot of water every day. Do research on how much your body specifically needs.

3. Wash your hands thoroughly a minimum of four times per day.

4. Keep your hands (and pens or pencils) away from your face and mouth.

5. Take a deep breath a minimum of four times per day.

6. Exercise four times a week with at least two cardio and two core workouts. Include five minutes of stretching after each workout session.

7. The Bible talks about being "anxious for nothing." Train yourself in this daily. Don't take on fear; instead, take on the peace of God. Train yourself to be calm and relaxed, even in the midst of a storm. Don't hang around the junkyards of worry, fear, or anxious thoughts.

8. Read your Bible daily. Use it to develop a great PLA to retrain your thinking and paradigms. This also detoxes all the junk we've unfortunately been trained to believe.

9. Eat fruits and vegetables every single day.

10. Get a minimum of six-and-a-half to seven-and-a-half hours of sleep every night. However, if you feel yourself getting sick, ramp up your sleep for one week.

11. Educate yourself on what you eat, being well-informed to make wise choices.

CHAPTER TWELVE

Decision-making Checklist (3 types of decisions)

1. Major decision:

- Give it a minimum of ninety days before making that decision.
- Talk to three people from your wise counsel board. Meet them face-to-face and take notes. Go over the pros and cons. (Note: This is not a counseling session. Don't turn it into counseling for the same reason many people do: they want to have other people tell

them what to do so that when they do it and the counsel doesn't work out, then they have someone to blame.)

- Do diligent research, making great keynotes as you go.
- Use the "4-to-1 Rule."
- Confess over yourself that you have the wisdom of God and the leading of the Holy Spirit to see what you need to see and to have the understanding needed for that decision. Then receive it and believe it.
- Examine your choices to see if/how they align with biblical principles and the goals you set for each area of your life.
- Only after all that, I would recommend praying and fasting.
- Let your prayers align themselves with God's promises regarding that decision.
- Confess (believe and speak) that you know what to do based on God's wisdom and the leading of the Holy Spirit.
- Then take time to be still and quiet and listen to the "still small voice" of God in your spirit.
- Most importantly, don't be rushed!
- If you have a "check" in your spirit, do not go forward with that decision. Be led by the peace of God.

2. **Important decision:**

- Give it a minimum of thirty days.
- Talk to two people from your wise counsel board either face-to-face or by phone for at least twenty to thirty minutes. Go over all the pros and cons. Take notes. (Remember, this is not a counseling session.)
- Do an intermediate amount of research, not too heavy but not too light. Again, make useful keynotes of the facts.

- Use the "4-to-1 Rule."
- Confess over yourself that you have the wisdom of God and the leading of the Holy Spirit to make a quality decision. Then receive it and believe it.
- Examine your choices to see if/how they align with biblical principles and the goals you set for each area of your life.
- Spend some time in prayer, being still and quiet before God, listening to His voice.
- Then pray about it. Don't just ask God about it but firmly believe that He will show you which direction to go.
- Don't be in a rush to make the decision.
- Make sure you have a peace from God before moving forward with your decision.

3. **Small to intermediate decision:**

- Give it a minimum of one week.
- Talk to one or two people via telephone for approximately fifteen minutes, going over the facts and details and the pros and the cons.
- Do medium to light research, making keynotes as you go.
- Use the "4-to-1 Rule."
- Believe and confess over yourself, "I have the wisdom of God, and I am directed by His Holy Spirit."
- Examine your choices to see if/how they align with biblical principles and the goals you set for each area of your life.
- Then be still and quiet before God, and pray about that particular decision, listening to His voice.
- Make sure you have a peace from God before moving forward with your decision.

The Power of Letting Go

- Let go of toxic people in your life.
- Let go of your past mistakes.
- Let go of the need to be right.
- Let go of feeling sorry for yourself.
- Let go of negative self-talk.
- Let go of the need to impress others.
- Let go of average beliefs.
- Let go of trying to please everyone.
- Let go of complaining.
- Let go of worrying about the future.

CHAPTER THIRTEEN

The 11 Cornerstones

- Cornerstone 1 – Your Alignments
- Cornerstone 2 – Your Plan
- Cornerstone 3 – Your Thinking
- Cornerstone 4 – Your Disciplines
- Cornerstone 5 – Your Attitude
- Cornerstone 6 – Your Systems
- Cornerstone 7 – Your Resolve
- Cornerstone 8 – Your Accountability
- Cornerstone 9 – The 8 Areas of Your Life
- Cornerstone 10 – Your Work Ethic
- Cornerstone 11 – Thankfulness

CHAPTER FOURTEEN

The Top 15 Excuses

1. Someday, I might try . . . .
2. That's not me.
3. You don't understand.
4. It's not my fault.
5. I've tried that.
6. I don't have the money.
7. It's hard.

8. I don't have the time.
9. I'm tired.
10. I've never done that before.
11. What if . . . ?
12. What is the use?
13. I'm too old.
14. I don't understand.
15. That's so unfair.

CHAPTER FIFTEEN

The fruit of a person with no systematic, written plan

- Successful in one or two areas, but the rest are suffering
- Usually frustrated
- Often tired and complaining
- Inconsistent
- Lazy and lethargic
- Confined in financial jail, living week-to-week or month-to-month
- Riding an emotional roller coaster
- Messy home or car
- Average or poor relationships
- Destiny or purpose has not been defined
- Usually very negative
- Easily offended
- Disorganized
- Like a balloon, floating wherever the wind blows
- Stress and anxiety are their best friends
- Always feeling sorry for themselves
- Grumpy, irritable, and no fun to be around
- Possessing selfish tendencies most of the time
- Thinking and mind-set is influenced by the news

Time Management: Mapping Your Time

1. **Dedicated appointments:** These are the appointments that you schedule in advance for all *8*

Areas of your life. Dedicate a time for these, including a specific start and end time, e.g., from 1–2 p.m. Below are just a few examples of what I set as dedicated appointments:

- Work out (typically four times a week)
- L-O: this stands for lights on, lights off. (Many overachievers don't recognize that the proper amount of sleep improves overall performance.)
- Sit down for breakfast, lunch, and/or dinner with my wife (typically five meals a week)
- Read
- Football games
- Ride my motorcycle
- Goal planning
- Business appointments
- PLA
- Prayer time
- Strategic wealth planning (Most people don't set appointments for themselves to build wealth. What do they end up doing? Working for money.)

2. **EGT list:** The second area of mapping is the to-do list, which I keep in my Notes app. I call it an EGT list, which stands for "Expect Great Things." The individual items on this list do not have their own dedicated appointment; however, I set dedicated appointments to accomplish tasks on the list.

I rank them in order of priority using the letters A, B, and C. Obviously, A is the highest priority. I never try to remember anything, as I typically have at least two hundred items or more on my EGT list. My goal is to complete five items each day. They range from books I want to read, to people I want to call or meet, to specific action items for my businesses and personal life.

When I am in the field with one of my businesses, I carry a clipboard with me in case I need to make notes to add to my EGT. (Sometimes, it's easier to write it down first and then add it to my phone later, especially when I'm talking with someone.)

3. **Goals:** There are hundreds of books written on goal planning. All of them carry a measure of truth and can be somewhat good for you. I believe the system put together in this book can be a gigantic game changer in your life when you discipline yourself to follow it for ninety consecutive days. We will explain this in more detail as we discuss your goals program (goal planning) and how much dedicated time you should spend on it.

4. **Designated checklist:** This refers to following the checklists which I have already created and designated for particular appointments. For instance, when I exercise by myself, I have an exercise checklist that I follow. When I go out of town, I have a travel checklist, which includes what I pack. I also have a checklist of people I pray for each day of the month. Creating checklists for routine or frequent endeavors keeps you focused on the task set before you.

Time Management: Planning Your Goals

1. Spend fifteen minutes every evening looking at your dedicated appointments for the next day and upcoming week. Review what's coming up, decide if you need to add or subtract anything, and determine the specific times for those appointments. After that, review your EGT list and goals. (Normally reviewing and modifying my designated checklists becomes an action item on my EGT list.)

2. For approximately thirty minutes every Sunday evening, work on your dedicated appointments, EGT, and goals lists.

3. On the fifteenth of each month, spend about ninety minutes planning the upcoming month. Plan your dedicated appointments, EGT list, goals, and your designated checklists.

4. On the first Wednesday of each calendar quarter, work out a detailed plan for the next twelve months for your dedicated appointments, EGT list, goals, and your designated checklists. This takes me approximately four hours. During this time, I also fill out my "Quarterly Personal Assessment."

Gigantic ways to create more time in all 8 Areas

- Don't rush past the beginning.
- Learn the art of politely saying, "No, thank you."
- View your time as a seed.
- Meet with the CEO of the world and get God's direction.
- Treat each day as very important.
- Practice taking mini-vacations.
- Never speed when driving.
- Learn the art of delegation.
- Don't gossip, argue, or debate.
- Discipline yourself to get up earlier and go to bed earlier.
- Exercise a minimum of four times a week.
- Practice the *15 Healthy Habits*.
- Look for ways to speak fewer words.
- Limit how often you check your emails. (Turn off the option for push notifications.)
- Hire a personal assistant.
- Declutter your home and workspace.
- Set maximum time limits on phone calls.
- Use checklists for all *8 Areas* to keep you focused and efficient. It will make your life easier.
- Put everything back in its place.
- Limit the time you watch TV. (This is big!)

- Limit how long you surf the web.
- Set time limits for all social media.
- Don't be in a rush.
- Don't wait until the last minute to get ready.
- Use travel time productively.
- Be cognizant of when people are wasting your time.
- Read a minimum of four books annually, or even better, read six or seven.
- Have a mission statement for your life and reanalyze it each quarter.
- Invest five minutes each day in visualizing the impossible for each of the *8 Areas* of your life (for a total of eight days).
- Practice self-discipline.
- Prepare yourself ahead of time for your meetings.
- Leave early for appointments.

CHAPTER SEVENTEEN

Build a disciplined lifestyle.

- Ask God to help you.
- Prophesy over yourself. Every day, speak over yourself, "I am a disciplined person."
- *See* yourself as a disciplined person. Envision it. This is critically important.
- Comprehend the reality that without pain you will have no growth. Embrace the pain.
- Start one discipline each month. Only one—not ten, not five, not even two. Just one a month. This one discipline will give you confidence in many ways and avenues.
- Have a plan for what you're going to do regarding that one discipline. Write out the action plan.
- Be accountable to others for that one discipline. Have someone with whom you can stay accountable daily or weekly via email or text.

- Remember, one of God's favorite words is *practice*. What you're doing is practicing that one discipline each day. Don't give up hope if you fail. Just keep practicing.
- Take the first step and just do it—today. One day at a time. Today is your *big day*.

What are the striking benefits of a disciplined life? I've listed nineteen below.

1. There is purpose in all that you do each day.
2. You know which direction to go and which steps to take.
3. You have peace even in the midst of a storm.
4. This gives you confidence that, through Christ, there is nothing you cannot do.
5. Discipline will produce incredible blessings from God in your life.
6. You will see an abundance of greatness in all *8 Areas*.
7. Discipline will help produce the fruit of the Spirit: love, joy, peace, patience, kindness, goodness, faithfulness, gentleness, and self-control.
8. Discipline will turn your dreams into reality.
9. Discipline allows you to have a healthy lifestyle along with an effective exercise program.
10. Discipline will give you the freedom of choice and the freedom to have a life of fulfillment.
11. The benefits of discipline will put you in a position to be "in a position."
12. Discipline will always put the odds in your favor.
13. Your life will be a light on the hill for all to see.
14. Discipline keeps you from wasting time.
15. Being disciplined will attract other disciplined people into your life, which will further motivate you.
16. Discipline transitions you from being conformed to this world to being transformed by God.
17. Discipline helps you avoid following the crowd.

18. The combined benefits of a disciplined life will help you reach your high calling.
19. Bottom line: discipline helps you tame your feelings and emotions.

CHAPTER NINETEEN

Systems that establish a platform of growth

1. Build a Keynote Book with eight different sections.
2. Use "Wisdom's Checklist of the Past" on page 61.
3. Practice focusing on living in the right time zone.
4. When your world turns upside down, bring out "The Big Guns" checklist on page 75.
5. Review the ingredients of a bad decision on pages 77-78 and practice avoiding them.
6. Review the ingredients of a wise decision on pages 78-79 and start practicing them.
7. Review the "5 Most Important Questions" to ask yourself each day on page 85-86, and practice asking yourself these questions daily.
8. Review the list of affirmations on pages 86-88. Develop your personal list of affirmations, and practice speaking them over yourself.
9. Practice using the *15 Healthy Habits* on page 91.
10. Practice using the "Decision-Making Checklist" (for the three types of decisions) on pages 98-100.
11. Build your wise counsel board.
12. Practice the points on "The Power of Letting Go" checklist on page 107.
13. Review the *11 Cornerstones* on page 112. Cornerstones 1–5 are your vehicle, or the way your life is progressing. Practice developing the condition of this vehicle. Add the fuel of Cornerstones 6–11 to your vehicle.
14. Review the Top 15 Excuses on page 120 and remove them from your vocabulary.
15. Practice aligning yourself with the Top 10 Spiritual Alignments on pages 121-125.

16. Change your thinking: develop a ferocious Powerful Learning Agenda (PLA), creating and implementing dedicated appointments for what you put on your list.
17. Practice effective time management: map out the *8 Areas* of your life according to the four areas listed on pages 132-134.
18. Start scheduling your dedicated appointments.
19. Start developing your Expect Great Things (EGT) list.
20. Implement the four areas of time planning found on pages 134-135.
21. Practice the "Gigantic ways to create more time in all *8 Areas*" listed on page 139.
22. Use the "Above and Beyond" goal plan on page 144.
23. Use the "Blueprint Contract" goal plan on page 145.
24. Track your growth by using the "Quarterly Personal Assessment" on page 146.
25. Remind yourself of the benefits of a disciplined life found on pages 157-158.

CHAPTER TWENTY

Top 18 Ways to Handle Adversity

1. Ask God for wisdom to solve the opportunity. Speak life over the opportunity. Don't rehearse the problem over and over.
2. Don't look for an easy fix. Don't be in a rush to get a quick solution just so you don't have to think about it anymore. You want a real solution, not a Band-Aid.
3. Be calm and collected, not emotionally too high or low. Be relaxed and at peace.
4. Put together a plan of action. Also, come up with Plan B and Plan C.
5. Ask God to help you. This sounds so simplistic, but you must realize that you were not designed to *be* God, so stop acting like you were. You're not God, but He is there to help you. Just ask and receive.

6. Evaluate the root of the opportunity. Be very honest with yourself. Address it analytically and objectively.

7. Set realistic expectations of solutions and time frames.

8. Switch or change your perspective. Don't look at it the same way but approach it from another angle.

9. Don't let the problem (opportunity) harass you. Most importantly, do not bring it to the dinner table or to bed. This is critical.

10. Set a dedicated appointment for focusing on that opportunity. Don't think about it again until then. If you need to set a second, third, or fourth appointment, then go ahead.

11. Don't let the adversity define who you are.

12. Forgive yourself and anyone else involved. Don't be critical, judgmental, or condemning toward yourself and others. Do not sit there and beat yourself up. Never gossip.

13. If you're presented with several opportunities at the same time, then sort them into groups: opportunity one, opportunity two, and so forth.

14. Understand that God has unprecedented favor for your life. See it, speak it, and receive it.

15. Put together a solid PLA regarding your opportunity. Without a doubt, there is *no way* I could have made it through countless difficult nights and days without depending totally upon the Word of God.

16. Approach it with a team. Put together a strategic team of big thinkers, which could also include your wise counsel board. Surround yourself with great team members. I would not be where I am today without phenomenal team members. (Note: this is not about a counseling session.)

17. Allow yourself to laugh about that opportunity and laugh at yourself.

18. Stay in shape physically during the opportunity.

CHAPTER TWENTY-ONE

Simple accountability measures that create great leaders

- Drive the speed limit all the time.
- Focus on driving the vehicle without being distracted by other devices.
- Never drive under the influence of drugs or alcohol.
- Always be honest with your taxes.
- Always be honest with an insurance claim.
- Treat other people the way you would want to be treated.
- Never take advantage of someone's lack of experience or education.
- Honor your father and mother.
- Wear your seatbelt.
- Don't partake of illegal drugs.
- Always tell the truth.
- Pay your bills on time.
- Honor your promises.
- Approach all transactions, whether personal or business, with integrity.
- Eradicate vulgar or foul language from your vocabulary.
- Be on time. It's a simple but very important part of accountability.

My top 10 accountability systems and tools

1. The scale. Be consistent about checking your weight.
2. Fill out a personal and business financial statement each quarter. (You can get this from your bank.)
3. Ask your spouse three things you can do to improve. Revisit that at least twice a month.
4. Ask your superiors three things you can do to improve. Visit with them at least once a quarter.
5. Exercise a minimum of four times a week.
6. Read a minimum of three hours a week.

7. Ask God what you could do better. Then take time to be quiet with Him, listening to how He answers you.
8. Share the gospel or pray with someone at least one time each month. Be an encouragement.
9. Go one week per month without television.
10. The famous "Mr. Budget" is a very practical means of accountability. Spend less than what comes in. The purpose of a budget is to build wealth.

CHAPTER TWENTY-THREE

How to win big on your week-ups

- Establish a work ethic in all *8 Areas* of your life.
- Have a simple plan, not jam-packed.
- Don't overextend your weekends with your to-do list. You're not in a weekend race!
- Train yourself to be quiet and turn off all distractions, especially all electronic devices, in order to develop a quiet mind-set. Retrain your paradigm of what rest and relaxation look like.
- Limit excessive eating; instead, eat extremely healthy food and quantities. (Having said that, I like to eat a somewhat unhealthy meal once a weekend or so, just not in excess.)
- Abstain from alcohol, TV, and (if you're like me, this is going to be tough) sports all weekend.
- Take a walk of at least one to five miles.
- Make time to think intentionally.
- Do something totally different or out of the ordinary.
- Build a vision board for all *8 Areas* of your life. This includes pictures that reflect what you envision in every area. Cut or print them out and post them where you can see them every day. Whatever it is you want—like a more peaceful life, more sales for your business, or better health—a vision board adds the color to your vision.
- Keep a gratitude journal. This is so, so important.

- Do one thing per weekend that will produce excellence in your life.
- If you have a Monday-through-Friday desk job, then do something physical on the weekends, like plant a small garden, wash your car by hand, or even do simple exercises. Some people's idea of physical exercise is filling up the bathtub, getting in it, unplugging the drain, and fighting the current. (That's a joke.)
- Practice releasing everything—every single care, every single anxious thought and feeling—to our God. I practice this for at least thirty minutes on Saturday or Sunday. It's like being on vacation for a week.
- Do something nice for your neighbor or friend.
- Volunteer for a great cause. But it's very, very important not to volunteer in excess.
- Write a letter at least once a month to somebody you admire and mail it to them. The fun part is trying to get their address.
- Meet one new person each month, especially in your neighborhood.
- Have some romantic time with your spouse. Make it fun.
- Crash someone's wedding! Just kidding.
- Prepare for your upcoming week.
- Work on your wealth plan.
- At least once a weekend, have adult playtime without alcohol or sports.
- Declutter your life. Practice the art of saying, "No, thank you."
- Practice smiling throughout the weekend.
- I've said it before, but I'm going say it again: limit your alcohol intake, or avoid it altogether. It really does not help you relax—just the opposite. We do not need alcohol to have fun, but we've been trained to believe that we do. For example, there was a time

when I thought it was impossible to have a great tailgate without alcohol. But it's just not the case! I really enjoy the game so much more being 100 percent sober.

- Take time to rearrange and reshape your priorities and what's important to you.
- Decide that, from Friday at 5 p.m. to Monday at 5 a.m., you will not complain or say any ugly words, especially to your loved ones. Wear a rubber band around your wrist, and every time you do complain or say something ugly, pop yourself.
- Drive a different way to your destination and/or drive a different way home. This stimulates creativity.
- Take a minimum of fifteen minutes each weekend to praise God for what He's done in your life.
- Over the span of a year, some of my favorite things to do on weekends include: visiting the botanical garden, visiting different types of museums, spending some time at the library, going to a park, going to a musical, riding a bicycle, helping with a prison ministry, attending a cooking school, riding my motorcycle, doing creative writing, being a tourist in my own city, trying out a new restaurant, cooking something from scratch that I've never made before, sending at least two encouraging texts to someone, visiting the zoo, taking a nap, getting a full-body massage, and deep breathing and stretching.

Examples of work ethic

- Intentionally and strategically plan for a productive and restful evening or week-up.
- For some, it may take hard work and discipline to train yourself to unplug from everything. This especially includes your phone, computer, and television.

- Look at your finances and analyze what may need to change or be done. Review your investments and study others.
- Have meaningful conversations with your team members and find out their needs.
- Slow your pace.
- Give yourself absolute silence and do nothing for an extended period. Start with thirty minutes, then work your way up. (This one takes a lot of work for most people.)
- Take some time to reflect on your priorities, potentially eliminating some of the things you're doing now. Another way to say this is, stop the roller coaster of your life. Get off and examine why you're even on the roller coaster in the first place.
- Organize and remove some, or all, of the clutter in areas such as your car, pantry, kitchen, closets, garage, and filing system. You'll feel a lot better and clear-minded.
- Plan and organize certain events, like your vacations. It can be as simple as being a tourist in your own city or one nearby. Come up with strategies for events in different areas of your life.
- My all-time favorite work ethic is setting thirty minutes to an hour just to talk with God; this is life-transforming.
- Decide to be diligent in examining all *8 Areas* of your life. (The "Quarterly Personal Assessment" on page 146 is a great tool you can use to help you see where you are, so that you know where you're going. Fill it out once a quarter.)

Warrior Checklist

- Cast down any thought that opposes what God's Word says about your life or your team members' lives.

- Speak words of faith. Call forth those things that are not (yet) as though they were. (e.g., "I have the greatest work ethic of anyone I know.")
- Speak words that are always full of life. Refuse to let any words come out of your mouth that contradict your potential.
- Choose to put the right things in your mouth.
- Discipline your emotions — not letting your emotions rule over you, but taking authority over how your emotions affect you.
- Remain unoffendable. Discipline yourself never to be offended.
- Exercise a minimum of four times a week.
- Have a believing heart. Continue in faith even when it doesn't look like it's working. Never, ever, ever give up on this.

APPENDIX II

Beginning on the next page, you will find *The Big Day* forms found at the end of Chapter 15. I encourage you to print them out and use them regularly.

THE BIG DAY

Above and Beyond

Year:

_____

Area:

_____

1. _____

2. _____

3. _____

4. _____

5. _____

6. _____

7. _____

8. _____

9. _____

10. _____

THE BIG DAY
Blueprint Contract

THE GOAL: _____

What is important to you about this goal? _____

_____

List one person who knows about this goal: _____

List the obstacles: _____

_____

Describe in detail the steps for reaching this goal: _____

_____

I, _____, as of this date, _____, do promise to give myself to do everything at my disposal to achieve this goal set before me. It is my choice to commit effort, discipline, and planning to achieve this goal. I will achieve this goal no later than _____, and my signature is my word that this goal will be completed no later than this date.

Signature: _____ Date: _____

QUARTERLY PERSONAL ASSESSMENT

_____ QUARTER OF THE YEAR 20 _____

Evaluate yourself in the *8 Areas* of your life using the following grading system:

A = Performing at peak levels / going "above and beyond"
B = Doing a satisfactory or good job / accomplishing what needs to be done but not more than that
C = Average, simply going through the motions / maintaining
D = Failing at this time

Now, before starting this exercise — especially for the first time — recognize that you are currently in one of three phases in every area of your life: the beginning, the intermediate, or the mature. Choose the phase you believe you are currently in for each area, and then grade yourself on that area.

Area of Your Life	Current Phase	Grade
Spiritual		
Health		
Family/Friends		
Career/Job/School		
Financial		
PLA		
Rest		
Hobby/Fun		

SECTION ONE

[1] Matthew 5:14
[2] Matthew 5:16 AMP
[3] Galatians 5:22–23
[4] Matthew 19:26
[5] Romans 8:38–39
[6] Genesis 1:26
[7] Romans 8:37
[8] Deuteronomy 28:13
[9] Matthew 19:26
[10] Jude 1:20
[11] Proverbs 4:1, 5–7, 11–13, 22–23, 25–26 AMP
[12] Revelation 1:8
[13] Psalm 139:2–3
[14] Philippians 4:7 NKJV
[15] Proverbs 4:5
[16] 1 Corinthians 9:24–27
[17] John 15:13
[18] 3 John 1:2
[19] "Biography," http://www.biography.com.
[20] Genesis 1:27
[21] John 10:10
[22] Romans 12:9 NLT
[23] Philippians 3:13 NASB
[24] 1 Samuel 17:36 AMP
[25] Hebrews 2:14–15 NIV
[26] James 1:5–6

SECTION TWO

[27] "practice," Dictionary.com,
http://www.dictionary.com/browse/practice.

28 James Clear, "How Long Does it Actually Take to Form a New Habit? (Backed by Science)," http://jamesclear.com/new-habit.

29 Romans 4:17 NKJV

30 Psalm 23:4 NKJV

31 Romans 8:28

32 Philippians 4:8 AMP

33 3 John 1:2 NKJV

34 Isaiah 54:17

35 Psalm 23:1

36 2 Timothy 1:7

37 Philippians 4:19

38 1 Peter 5:7

39 Joshua 1:9

40 1 John 5:4

41 Romans 8:38–39

42 Genesis 1:26

43 John 15:13; 1 John 3:16

44 Galatians 5:22–23

45 Ephesians 6:11

46 Isaiah 54:17

47 Philippians 4:6 NKJV

48 Ibid.

49 Hebrews 11:1 NKJV

50 1 Kings 19:12

51 1 Corinthians 13:4–7 AMP

52 Jeremiah 29:11 NKJV

53 John 14:27

SECTION THREE

54 Romans 4:17 NKJV

55 Psalm 18:32 NKJV

56 Psalm 18:34 NASB

57 Luke 18:27 NKJV

58 Proverbs 18:21

[59] John 15:13

[60] Proverbs 21:5 AMP

[61] Romans 12:2 NIV

[62] 1 Corinthians 2:16 AMP

[63] Philippians 4:8 AMP

[64] Proverbs 18:21

[65] Galatians 5:22–23

[66] Matthew 19:26 AMP

[67] Matthew 6:33 NASB

[68] Colossians 3:1–2 AMP

[69] "system," Dictionary.com,
http://www.dictionary.com/browse/system.

[70] 1 Peter 5:7 CEV

[71] 2 Corinthians 11:23–27 AMP

[72] 2 Corinthians 12:9 AMP

[73] 1 John 4:4 NASB

[74] James 1:2–6 AMP

[75] Exodus 34:28 AMP

[76] Luke 12:48

[77] Genesis 1:26

[78] Galatians 4:7

[79] Revelation 1:6, 5:10

[80] Ephesians 3:17

[81] Proverbs 21:5 NKJV

[82] 1 Corinthians 13:1

Made in the USA
Lexington, KY
18 March 2018